Artwork of the Mind

**An Interdisciplinary Description
of Insight and the Search for
it in Student Writing**

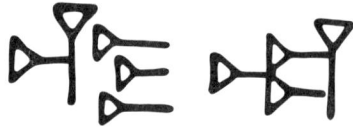

WRITTEN LANGUAGE
S E R I E S

Marcia Farr, editor

Collaboration and Conflict: A Contextual Exploration
   of Group Writing and Positive Emphasis
      Geoffrey Cross

Literacy: Interdisciplinary Conversations
      Deborah Keller-Cohen (ed.)

Literacy Across Communities
      Beverly Moss (ed.)

Validating Holistic Scoring for Writing Assessment:
   Theoretical and Empirical Foundations
      Michael Williamson and Brian Huot (eds.)

Artwork of the Mind: An Interdisciplinary Description
   of Insight and the Search for it in Student Writing
      Mary Murray

forthcoming

Perspectives on Written Argument
      Deborah Berrill (ed.)

Historical Considerations of Technical Communication
      John C. Brockmann

Subject to Change:
   New Composition Instructors' Theory and Practice
      Christine Farris

Portfolios and College Writing
      Liz Hamp-Lyons and William Condon

The Language of Professional Writing
      Kathryn Riley and Frank Parker

Computers and the Non-Native Writer:A Natural Partnership
      Martha C. Pennington

Twelve Readers Reading: Responding to College Student Writing
      Ronald Lunsford and Richard Straub

Artwork of the Mind
An Interdisciplinary Description of Insight and the Search for it in Student Writing

Mary Murray
Penn State-Hazleton

HAMPTON PRESS, INC.
CRESSKILL, NEW JERSEY

Printed in the United States of America

Library of Congress Cataloging-in-Publication Data

Murray, Mary, 1957-
    Artwork of the mind : an interdisciplinary description of insight and the search for it in student writing / Mary Murray.
        p.   cm -- (Written language)
    Includes bibliographical references and indexes.
    ISBN 1881303-63-2. -- ISBN 1-881303-64-0 (pbk.)
    1. Insight. 2. Insight--Testing. 3. Insight--Study and teaching (Higher) 4. Rhetoric and psychology. I. Title. II. Series: Written language series.
BF449.5M87   1995
153.4--dc20   95-6445
                                                                    CIP

Hampton Press, Inc.
23 Broadway
Cresskill, NJ 07626

Cover design: Karen Siletti
Artist: Zehna Barros

For

Florence Gucwa

and

Kathy, JoAnn, Lisa, Chris, Sandy, Becky, . . .

Contents

Series Preface

Marcia Farr, Series Editor

This new series examines the characteristics of *writing* in the human world. Volumes in the series present scholarly work on written language in its various contexts. Across time and space, human beings use various forms of written language—or writing systems—to fulfill a range of social, cultural, and personal functions, and this diversity can be studied from a variety of perspectives within both the social sciences and the humanities, including those of linguistics, anthropology, psychology, education, rhetoric, literary criticism, philosophy, and history. Although writing is not often used apart from oral language, or without aspects of reading, and thus many volumes in this series include other facets of language and communication, writing itself receives primary emphasis.

This particular volume focuses entirely on writing, especially on the role of insight in composing processes. Although insight is a notion that enjoys wide understanding, it is extraordinarily difficult to define and study. This volume synthesizes the literature on insight from a variety of disciplines, including especially theology and psychology, and innovatively suggests a methodology for studying it. Because insight is generally agreed to be an important aspect of learning as well as of composing, advances in our concrete understandings of how it operates in the teaching and learning of writing are particularly welcome.

While the study of writing is absorbing in its own right, it is an increasingly important social issue as well, as demographic movements occur around the world and as language and ethnicity accrue more intensely political meanings. Writing, and literacy more generally, is central to education, and education in turn is central to occupational and social mobility. Manuscripts that present either the results of empirical research, both qualitative and quantitative, or theoretical treatments of relevant issues are encouraged for submission.

Acknowledgments

The patience of certain people made this book a reality, most notable of whom is Dr. J. William Asher who allowed me to pour and puzzle over *Psychometric Theory* for a whole summer. I'm grateful for the advice of Dr. Don Brown, my statistics teacher, who helped structure my project, and Drs. Janice Lauer and Pat Sullivan who advised the genesis of this book in my dissertation.

The advice and wisdom of Dr. Carol Camp Yeakey guided me through the initial stages of this book, and I'm forever grateful. Dr. Kathy Rowan's encouragement, warmth, and specific comments on Chapter 4 I'm especially thankful for.

My poet colleagues Drs. Chris Millis and Diane Stevenson always understood about insight and working with them was a treasure. For their advice simply on writing, Drs. Linda Robertson and Jane Danielwicz taught me much. For always understanding and appreciating the beauty of numerical matters, there is no colleague like Dr. Dianne Atkinson.

There is no one at Purdue when I was developing these instruments who didn't help—thank you all.

Series Editor Marcia Farr, Publisher Barbara Bernstein, and Diana Dulaney were marvelous to work with: their comments shaped the book well and their support was unfailing. Cover artist Zehna Barros was very generous with her time and talent.

Many thanks to the students who volunteered their efforts: Sarajane Highmore, Todd Weiss, Troy Funk, Mark Davis, Doris, and many other students whose work and insights began this study.

Who can count the value of friends who listen and encourage and badger me to finish? Thanks go to John Leonard, Jane and Carl Molodetz, Pauline and Joe Jennings, Brother Augie Jackson OCSO, Penny Riggs, Paul Weingartner, Julie Farrar, Ruth Porritt, Al Witkowski, Steve Pierson, my dear mom who reads everything I write, my grandmother the cheerleader, and the whole Cleveland crew.

Introduction:
The Silent Request
for Insight

PROLOGUE

It is the fall semester at a small liberal arts college and three first-year students read their writing assignments. In political science, Alex is asked to compare and contrast two theorists in the space of five pages. In general education, Mike is told to compare and contrast three tribes Margaret Mead studied and provide comparisons to "American culture." In economics, Carrie is expected to discuss several methods of analysis.

Each of the students presented and counterposed information for five pages, and each received an almost failing score. Having taken the assignment literally, each student recognized in the low score that there was another assignment, an implicit one, a silent request for insight.

Noted commentators on higher education believe that the lack of insight is at the heart of the problems of this institution. Ernest Boyer (1987) and others call for integration and synthesis within and between college courses; historian Page Smith

1

(1990) cited the paucity of student academic life. What might insight look like for these three students and why is it so crucial to their higher education?

My work with these faculty in writing workshops and in consultations made me privy to their unstated goals. What the political science professor really wanted was for Alex to relate the theorists to the present day political economy; had Alex done so, he might have been more adept at analyzing current and future events. What the general education professor really wanted from Mike was that he look closely at gender roles and how they are constructed in our society; had Mike done so he would have asked himself important questions about his own upbringing. What the economics professor really wanted was for Carrie to judge the kinds of knowledge produced by methods in economics; had she made such judgments she would have been able to ask important questions about research in this field.

Instead of making connections and evaluations, these students reported information, and in so doing, lost much more than a good grade. Each of these assignments points students toward responsible membership in the academic community and beyond. Not entering in to the assignment at a greater depth actually causes students to remain in a spectator role. Yet, this role is chosen not willfully but out of ignorance.

The connections and evaluations professors desire are not the product of gathering information, but of integrating information with the students' emotions, experiences, and attitudes. Not integrating these things not only prevents connections and evaluations from being made, but also leaves students without the chance to engage in real scholarship. In short, without integration, everyone loses: Professors lose the ability to dialogue with students because they express no opinion, evaluation, or connections; students lose a chance to develop skills of scholarship; the academic community loses members; and society has fewer insightful workers and thinkers.

Definition of Insight

Insight is an understudied construct in its home discipline of psychology, therefore the definition that follows has as its base a synthesis of interdisciplinary findings that are discussed at length in Chapter 2.

Insight is a type of understanding that results when a person resolves a meaningful dissonance (lack of harmony) through integrating experiences, attitudes, or emotions with the intellect in such a way that the particular resolution is a simple, permanently true, powerful personal knowledge that is used to interpret other dissonances past and future.

Contrasting insight with other forms of knowing, its unique nature rests in the inner world of the person that enables insight to happen and in the mysterious, little understood process of synthesis that crystallizes so much information into a maxim. Defined as such, it is clear that insight is a form of knowing, as well as a form of creativity. Popular understanding links creativity and insight, yet they are not the same. *Creativity* is the general term for generating that which is novel; insight is a particular kind of novelty. Creativity does not always yield the synthesis and integration that insights do, neither does it always yield a resolution to dissonance. Another kind of confusion in popular understanding involves the term itself. Insight can commonly mean a quick solution coming from out of the blue. The qualities of speed and effortlessness get foregrounded and distract us away from the missing aspects that true insights have. A quick, easy solution, like opening a locked vehicle, does not integrate various parts of the person simply because they are not called into question. The solution is not one that is powerful and used in the future to interpret other events. Nevertheless, such solutions are just as important as insights: imagine if a child were locked in the car. Insights are not better than other forms of understanding, they simply differ in how they are achieved and in their rich qualities.

Insights are had under certain circumstances; when professors incorporate those circumstances into education, there will be more insights. In order to best describe the facets of the insight experience I have organized my interdisciplinary findings chronologically into the prerequisites, qualities, and aftereffects of insight.

Let us begin with the *prerequisites*. Before insights are had, there must be deep human dissonance or puzzlement, be it conscious or unconscious. People can live for years without recognizing this discomfort, and subsequently, they never have any insights. It is the recognition and confrontation of this dissonance (lack of harmony) that leads us to confront or question, and out of this step toward the unknown, insight can come.

No one knows, not even cognitive psychologists who claim to study insight, the mechanisms of insight in the human mind; yet, that an insight has occurred is readily agreed on by psychologists and laypeople alike. Indeed, once an insight has occurred and the person verifies it (through experience, by consulting others, or with the passage of time), certain *qualities* prove identifiable to label the insight experience in retrospect. Chief among these qualities, according to scholars from all disciplines, is the type of understanding: It is a radically new vision that is a simple and permanent solution to the preceding dissonance. Insight involves the full human person (intellect plus emotions, attitudes, intuition, experience, and culture) and displays some of our deepest values. A further quality of insight is that it exposes our limits of knowledge: Insights frequently point to areas we need to develop in order to more fully resolve a concern of ours.

The *effects* of insight are worth all the struggle and even infinite waiting that we might incur. Insights often yield direction and therefore action; they bring peace where once there was confusion; the mind keeps pouring over an insight, gleaning more and more from it as time goes by; and we own insights personally and bring them to bear on events past and future, often distilling them into maxims that we hold dear.

PURPOSE

This volume presents an interdisciplinary description of the construct of insight and two measurement instruments for identifying insight in writing that are based on this description. The purpose of this study is to enable researchers and teachers to identify and foster insight at the college level in writing assignments within and beyond composition courses.

Definitions of Writing that Prohibit Insight

Why don't professors ask for insight? They want it, but their implicit definition of writing may not include it. Broadly considered, writing must include both inquiry (or the thinking, reading, research, intuiting, and feeling required to answer a question) and communication (the organization and articulation of the answer for some audience). When writing is reduced to the second of these parts, as is commonly done, insight cannot be readily expected.

The common misperception that writing is largely a matter of style and grammatical correctness and that some students are "gifted" with verbal ability and some not stems from a reliance on a 19th century romantic model of writing. It results from the schism in the early 1600s when logic was separated from rhetoric by Pierre de la Rameé. Since the 1960s, scholars of rhetoric have addressed this schism, enhancing composition pedagogy with sophisticated inquiry patterns designed to increase the quality of thought in student writing. Nevertheless, the field of composition studies is relatively young, and the fruits of its scholarship are not known to enough of the academic community. Thus, it is entirely plausible that the professors mentioned earlier had never heard or thought that the writing process requires inquiry as well as communication.

How does this model of writing based on communication alone inhibit insight? It turns students' attention to the surface features of a text, not to the content. It can preclude reflection, intuition, and emotion in favor of a well-organized argument that remains outside the students' own interests and questions. It places students outside the very situation that encourages insight; the confrontation of a complex and meaningful dissonance with the full human person is reduced to a request for the isolation of theoretical, abstract, or factual "knowledge." When writing is considered a matter of style and grammar alone (with the fervent but silent hope for insight from only the "gifted") it can produce profound separation between professor and student and reduce instead of raise the intellectual stature of the student.

All students, especially the weakest, have profound questions. As theologian Paul Tillich put it, insight is never an abstract, theoretical matter; it arises from human questions in a particular context. If we want insight, there can be no consideration of writing as merely surface features or as a vehicle of information.

Defining Writing to Encourage Insight

If writing is comprised of both inquiry and communication concerns, how might we define good writing? Good writing exhibits ideas that are well thought out, well researched, deeply felt and intuited, whereas the text itself is aimed toward a particular audience, is well organized, and displays appropriate style and correct grammar. Although many writing pedagogies exist to assist writers in adapting to audiences, organizing texts, polishing style, and correcting grammar, few have been designed to foster the most mysterious, and yet desired, aspect of writing at the collegiate level—that of insight.

We know what an insightful paper is intuitively. It is one that expresses not only information regarding the topic at hand, but also synthesizes that information in an original and thoughtful way. The writer of that essay is known for his or her opinion: It is not a generic student essay. There is a depth and originality to it that separates it from the average paper. What insight in writing means, in brief, is that the writer has confronted a complex and meaningful dissonance with his or her intellect as well as his or her attitudes, emotions, experiences, intuition, memory, and culture, and in so doing the writer is aware of the appearance of meaning that resolves the dissonance fully.

Why College Teachers Should Encourage Insight in Writing

Our society would benefit from the inclusion of insight in college-level writing for a number of reasons. Ernest Boyer (1987), author of *College: The Undergraduate Experience in America,* proposed that language be "the first requirement" in refashioning our colleges and universities to be intellectual strongholds for our culture. As he said:

> Writing holds us responsible for our words and ultimately makes us more thoughtful human beings. As students put their ideas on paper, they improve their understanding and discover both the discipline and joy of self-expression. Guided by a good teacher, all students can become better writers, and in the process thinking becomes more precise. (pp. 78-79)

In our postindustrial society, students who are trained to use writing as a means to insight will offer their workplaces far greater gifts than they do as students who merely repeat others' ideas.

Robert Reich (1992), former Harvard political economist and current Secretary of Labor, made this same point. He stated that 35% to 40% of Japan's workers are trained to be "symbolic analysts" or problem solvers. The United States can claim less than half this amount because our workers are severely undertrained and undervalued for their own problem-solving abilities. Reich called for a $2 million investment in education to make U.S. workers able to compete with the changing needs of a global market. Reich's recommendation points not only to the importance of training in business operations, but also to training in insight.

Encouraging insight in college writing will be particularly helpful to women. Belenky, Clinchy, Goldberger, and Tarule (1986), in *Women's Ways of Knowing*, said that much of women's knowledge is from experience and intuition and that such ways of knowing are undervalued (if not scorned) in academe. Insight links the personal with more traditional or factual studies. An example a young woman's insight in writing follows in Chapter 6; in her advanced economics course (a seminar on Thorstein Veblen) she uses Veblen's theory of the leisure class to explain her compulsive purchasing of lingerie at Victoria's Secret. The essays I have seen wherein a student links these two domains of knowing produce very powerful insights that change behavior.

Because insight calls forth the values of the individual, it has the potential to deeply enhance the learning experience of minorities in particular. I cannot help but wonder how much wisdom goes unheeded or is suppressed, or worse yet, is completely abandoned when minorities feel they cannot share their insights in writing. Matthew Fox (1988), a theologian, wrote that our spiritually bankrupt age needs the infusion of the wisdom of those most dissociated from it—the Native American, the female, the African American, the poor. Reworded, we may be privileged to receive the wisdom from many traditions if students are encouraged to use writing as a means to insight.

The opposite of insight is not ignorance, but isolation, despair, and frustration. Thus, a fourth reason for encouraging insight through college writing is to reduce isolation between student and professor. When students perceive an assignment to be a request to repeat either the teacher's point of view or information they have read, they resist and isolate themselves in tepid essays. These assignments do not call forth the responses of persons; they ask for preordained answers, and students respond with rebellion or withdrawal. The paradox exists that the more we express ourselves individually, the more possibility for dialogue; the more hiding in boring essays, the less chance for dialogue and insight. Insight is artwork of the mind, and like most artwork, it calls forth a response.

AN APPROACH TO THE STUDY OF INSIGHT

Some Basic Assumptions

Most research about assessing writing has been conducted using holistic scoring, which assigns one rating to a text (usually an essay) that corresponds to its overall quality. The holistic assessment of writing is commonly understood as a way to determine to what extent a text will meet societal expectations of written texts; a high holistic score is one that reflects our culture's values on clarity, correctness, thoroughness, and consistency. In contrast to this kind of assessment, which stresses the worth of writing to society at large, this study assumes that insight in writing is intrinsically interesting and merits study in its own right, without trying to merge it with other features of a text.

Nevertheless, when holistic scoring is used for research purposes, it "blurs any distinctions" that the researcher wishes to study (Quellmalz, 1981). Even analytic scoring, which separates out various features of a text for holistic scoring, retains the blurring. In the analytic scoring system of Diederich (1974) for instance, the closest feature of writing to insight is that of quality of ideas. Yet, quality of ideas could as easily refer to the complexity of ideas as to their synthesis. No other measures exist to isolate insight in writing, although various researchers point out the need for such measures. Odell (1981), defining writing competence as the ability to discover what one wishes to say, contended that "the role of discovery in the process of composition has an important bearing on the limitations of existing procedures for measuring writing ability and provides the key to improving the ways we evaluate students' competence as writers" (p. 100). White (1985), considering English an individualizing discipline, spoke of the responsibility to help students "present individual, original ideas" and "develop a sense of identity through reading and writing" (p. 10). But he lamented that "both the teaching and the testing of English as an individualizing discipline are difficult and frequently unwelcome" (p. 15). The assumption that insight in writing deserves an isolated analysis places this study in the tradition of psychometrics.

Measurement theory rests on a relationship established between numbers and their assignment to objects or events according to a set of rules (Kerlinger, 1986, p. 329). Although a construct is not directly measurable—like leadership, interdependence, or insight—the researcher can measure it if the construct is described thoroughly. Another assumption of this study is that the interdisciplinary description of insight is thorough enough to support measurement efforts.

Assigning Numbers to Insight

The measurement instruments presented in this volume assign numbers to insight in different ways. The scale assigns a number to an expressive essay, the test for a self-report of experience.

Insight Scale.

This scale assigns a number to the degree to which a writer has resolved a dissonance in an expressive essay. This kind of essay most visibly manifests the insight experience. In order to devise this measurement instrument, more than 200 expressive essays written by first-year students enrolled in composition at a large midwestern university were intuitively sorted into piles of "insightful" and "not insightful" writing. The essays were analyzed for insight using the interdisciplinary description. Rather than isolate one part of the writing, such as the conclusion, to be analyzed, the entire essay was used. The goal of the analysis was to identify and describe various levels of dissonance resolution. The sortings, combined with descriptions of insight from several disciplines, yielded the scale found in Chapter 3.

Insight Test.

This Likert-type questionnaire assigns a number to the degree to which students report having had an insight experience after writing an assignment. Unlike the expressive essay, most college writing assignments do not manifest the writer's experiences, and thus insight in these texts is not visible; nevertheless, that the experience has taken place is what the questionnaire seeks to uncover. In order to devise this questionnaire, a variety of wordings and item types corresponding to the interdisciplinary description of insight were written and given to student volunteers. The Likert-type item corresponded most accurately to students' reports of insight experiences. A large set of items (140) was screened for quality by an even larger number of students (n = 566) to create the 30-item questionnaire found in Chapter 4.

AN OVERVIEW

The following chapters are briefly described here. Taken together, they provide specific tools and suggestions for including insight in college-level writing.

In Chapter 1, "Insight as an Academic Pursuit," the goals of varying disciplines are outlined regarding insight studies. Knowledge of the motivation underlying these studies is essential to understanding the limits and assets of each field's contributions.

Chapter 2, "The 16 Dimensions of Insight," presents features of insight agreed by scholars in a variety of disciplines. The accord of their findings provides the domain from which I design my measurement instruments.

Chapter 3, "A Scale for Insight," provides a scale for assessing dissonance resolution in student writing. This scale can only be applied to expressive writing, the principle aim of which is to manifest the thoughts and feelings of the writer. This type of writing most clearly illustrates the experience of insight; the scale describes what an insight looks like in expressive writing along with descriptions of incomplete, partial, or unattempted insights.

Chapter 4, "A Test for Insight," presents a second measurement instrument. Designed as a self-report Likert-type questionnaire, this test indicates whether writing one particular assignment increased the writer's understanding. Unlike the scale presented in Chapter 3, this instrument does not rely on any particular type of writing or on a human rater. It can be used, for instance, by a political science professor after students have completed a research paper; the measurement instrument would tell the professor whether students had insights as a result of writing that assignment.

In Chapter 5, "Encouraging Insight in Student Writing," a coherent pedagogical approach is suggested for encouraging insight in any college classroom. I also offer suggestions to enhance current practices. Samples of two students' work (with stages of composing) are included.

Chapter 6, "Insight, Mystery, and Art," discusses the nature of insight as mystery and proposes visual art as capable of yielding insight. Like the nature of light, the nature of insight is not fully understood. This chapter considers writers' descriptions of insight as mystery.

It also concerns insight as a function of art. When attempts at insight fail, several writers propose art as the next avenue. An appreciation of the mystery of insight (meaning its inscrutable appearance, often wondrous content, ability to unify, and its permanence) is encouraged in both writing and visual art.

1

Insight as an Academic Pursuit

Of the many, many essays carried home in worn briefcases by professors, far too many of them seem to be written by a generic student. The effort made by rhetoricians to breathe some humanity and thought into those essays is the same effort that spurred researchers across disciplines to study the nature of insight. Whereas the next several chapters are devoted to describing findings and to suggesting ways to foster insight in writing, this chapter provides the cultural and intellectual backdrop of insight studies. In an era in which our ways of knowing have come under important scrutiny, it is imperative to do so. In this way, limitations and new directions will be more apparent.

To summarize across disciplines, the study of insight is a quest for wholeness and responsibility. Psychologists wish clients to integrate their past or their feelings into their understandings in order that they be mentally healthy or whole; theologians validate the experience of inner awareness or insight as a kind of knowing that allows individuals to understand the fuller context of their lives; philosopher Lonergan examined insight as a form and ground of human knowing that is the key to acting freely and responsibly; and composition and rhetoric scholars, in their rediscovery of the ancient rhetoricians, reunite thinking and personal meaning with form and style, the latter two having reigned for centuries as the sole concerns of writing instruction. This focus on integration in each of these fields is an important future direction for higher education.

Insight and Psychology

Gene Glass (1986), a prominent psychological statistician, claimed that if any field holds out great hope for its possible con- tributions to mental health, it is research in psychoanalysis. Research that simplified important and widely used constructs, such as the self and insight, to name just two, would be quite valuable. Ironically, claimed Glass, important constructs used to describe our deepest human traits remain understudied or wrapped in an aura of statistics that belie an Oz without a wizard. Insight may be an enigmatic construct, but is it any more enig- matic than the state of a field that has no ready description for a term it uses constantly?

Insight studies have fallen victim to a split in the field between empiricists and clinicians, yet current economic condi- tions favor more work on insight. Empiricists probably would not have recently (in the last 10 years) undertaken the quantification of insight were it not for a great need in the clinical world. Clients referred to therapy who relied on government or insurance funds formerly obtained years of counseling sessions; however financial constraints have forced these agencies to reduce the number of sessions (Strupp & Binder, 1984). So that the fewest number of sessions promotes the greatest amount of help, researchers now try to determine which elements in a therapy session promote wholeness in the shortest amount of time. Elliott (1985) simu- lated such a setting with university students, requiring them to relate "helpful" and "nonhelpful" events. Insight turned out to be, as we might expect, quite a helpful event.

The recent focus on the quantification of insight does not mean that no one before now attempted it. In Chapter 3 a discus- sion of these attempts is presented. Most relevant here would be to note the paucity of such studies and even a call from one psycholo- gist (Wallerstein, 1983) for more research into the nature of the construct. The closest empiricists have come is a measure called *The Experiencing Scale* (Klein, Mathieu, Gendlin, &

Kiesler, 1969) that sets to seven levels the degree to which clients integrate their emotions into their reports of experiences. Current attempts grapple with operational definitions.

To summarize, empirical renditions of the construct of insight do not provide a solid understanding of its nature; that is not to say, however, that these studies should be discounted or considered unimportant steps toward our fuller understanding.

Theoretical accounts of insight, although few, are often rich. The work of Schafer (1978) and Shengold (1981) are examples. In his summary of insight literature, Roback (1974) related that although the term *insight* is widely used, he found its meaning "nebulous." The nature of the profession is a factor in the paucity of research: Clients are seen individually and few chances exist for large-scale studies. The bias against large-scale work also influences research in this area. Thus, a frequent treatment of insight in this literature is a case study instead of a long and thoughtful reflection from a seasoned therapist. Nonetheless, a few societal trends in insight interests are evident.

The 1960s have therapists arguing over "true" and "false" insight, claiming that action and cures denote true insights and that inaction and recurrent needs for solutions indicate false insights. The emphasis here, as to be expected, is on the health of the client, not on the insight experience itself. This retrospective vision of insight as curative was challenged two decades later by Wallerstein, who presented evidence of insight without change and change without insight. That is, there are clients who never have insights, yet show improvement in actions, in taking responsibility, and in personal peace of mind; there are also clients who have insights who show no sign of improvement. Thus, the role of insight in mental health is not yet clear, although as seen with Elliott's study, insight remains an important and helpful event in therapy.

The theoretical studies of psychologists in the 1970s and 1980s reveal the need for confrontation and the fact that insight is not likely to occur without it. One 10-year case study (Labov & Fanshel, 1970) illustrates this quite well. The few studies that exist do point to language as a key, whether in a metaphorical sense or in a literal rendering of the import of each statement in the therapeutic dialogue.

Like Glass and Wallerstein said, much work is needed both empirically and theoretically. The needs mandated by restricted government and insurance funds may be a key impetus.

Yet another set of psychologists, creativity researchers,

add to the literature on insight. Wallas (1926) was the first to map out in a linear sequence the creative process as one progressing from questioning and confusion to illumination. Much of this literature, however, concentrates not on insight itself but on novelty; insight gets lost amid fantastic solutions and perspective shifts. DeBono (1970, 1992), Koestler (1949), and Perkins (1981) offered effective strategies to begin the creative process. Nevertheless, what becomes confusing is that the strategies for novelty and perspective shifts detract from the unseen parts of the insight experience: the long and often unconscious dwelling on one's subject, the need to be curious, and how one confronts what is complex and barely understood. Creativity scholars, however, offer a way to insight that their colleagues in therapy can only describe after witnessing the event.

Insight and Theology

If theologians add one thing to the study of insight, it is their broader perspective regarding the experience. Unlike psychologists, they are not studying patients who are (at least) clinically mentally ill. They evaluate the insight experience in light of the entire context of an individual's life. Thus, their perspective augments that of psychologists. Nevertheless, no one could be more surprised at insight than theologians. Recovering (as most of our culture is) from three centuries of rationalism and empiricism, they are confronted with the insight experience as a way of personal knowing that was never sanctioned or validated until recently in the work of prominent theologians such as Rudolf Bultmann, Karl Rahner, and Paul Tillich.

It is important to understand how insight came to be so undervalued, if not feminized, by theologians. The experience of insight for them is considered revelation, although no one attempts to assign cause to either the individual or to the divine. The fact that an individual has an insight that yields knowledge that resolves issues in his or her life is not, at this time, explained by theologians—it is simply being verified and valued. It is as if the Zen enlightenment pattern were discovered in the 1960s by Western theologians.

The roots of the lack of acknowledgment of insight rest in Scholasticism and its understanding of revelation. Gregory Baum (1973), in tracing attitudes toward insight and revelation, claimed that the church of the counterreformation extended rationalist principles of the Scholastics, who considered religious truth an intellectual matter. "Sacred reality" was construed as independent of humans and history. This understanding is embodied in "dogma," or sacred reality intellectually rendered. This belief continued into the 19th century wherein revelation was considered "a series of truths" communicated through scripture and the church that were "inaccessible to man's intelligence." With faith a matter of the intellect, and God no longer mystery but an independent and almost abstract matter, revelation was reified in dogma and scripture and thus was removed from human experience.

Unfortunately, the notion of revelation as exclusively truth- and fact-centered persists. Baum (1973), Fox (1988), and O'Meara (1990) noted the rise of fundamentalism and literalism across the globe and saw it as the aftermath of this neo-Scholasticism.

Seeking to unearth revelation from its concrete and intellectual nature as seen in the past centuries, a number of prominent theologians consider revelation *new awareness* as Dulles (1985) termed it. In order to present two new directions in revelation studies, let me couch this discussion in terms of Karl Rahner's understanding of revelation because it encompasses both.

Rahner (1966), like Bultmann and Tillich, believes that revelation always has two parts: the experience of the transcendent and the historical event of that experience. In his Western Christian perspective, Rahner pinpointed the historical event as the Jewish man born in the first century in Nazareth; nevertheless the ideas he proposes fit for other cultures as well. He and Bultmann believe that too much emphasis has been placed on the historicity of the divine and far too little on the experience of transcendence, which is not restricted to set historical events. God, for Rahner, is the "living, permanent, transcendent ground of self-movement of the world itself" (p. 12). The key in Rahner's theory that explains insight experiences and fosters this emphasis in other theologians is that God is always communicating Godself because God is imminent. As prime mover, according to Rahner, no movement (or understanding) can take place without the divine. Thus, to understand revelation merely in terms of what the church dictates through dogma, what scripture says, or through set historical events is to deny the presence and action of God in the world and through human beings. In Rahner's viewpoint, insight is equally as valid as these traditional forms of knowledge.

Isolating insight from other types of revelation (e.g. *feeling* something of the divine) Avery Dulles articulated the benefits and struggles of this newer understanding. Questions of validity confront the insight as "new awareness" theologians; yet the quality of life and degree of knowledge had from an insight cannot be refuted. Their descriptions of the experience echo well and expand the descriptions of psychologists.

The second direction that modern theology finds itself headed toward with regard to insight is the renewed emphasis on the imagination. Storytelling and remythologizing also focus attention on the experience of insight as yielding knowledge. Storyteller, poet, and theologian John Shea believes we tell stories because they give us life; his writings consistently reveal stories that echo the insight experience described by psychologists. When he and other writers point readers toward imaginative experience, they frequently point them toward an experience of integration and insight.

Readers may find it surprising that theologians are returning to imaginative forms of writing when holy texts everywhere are comprised of stories. The shift taking place returns the experience of the divine to the individual.

Insight for Lonergan

Written in 1957, Bernard Lonergan's (1957/1978) book-length study *Insight* has been considered one of the major philosophical events of the 20th century. Frank P. Braio (1988), in an explication of Lonergan's work, related that Lonergan's original preface places him in the same search for wholeness that encompasses researchers in other disciplines.

Lonergan, said Braio, fully realized that in the middle of a century filled with wars, unprecedented destruction, fragmentation, and bewilderment unknown to prior ages, self-knowledge was no longer a private matter—it was a social crisis. Perhaps we can see Lonergan answering the questions pressing on millions: How can we act responsibly? Under what conditions do people make responsible decisions? What is the nature of our understanding, so that we can employ it for our own good?

Insight for Lonergan is but one type of human understanding. If, he reasoned, we understand how we understand, we touch the ground of our humanity and we are provided with a "fixed base" from which to view subsequent developments of thinking no matter what the endeavor.

If we are to be intelligent and rational, responsible and free, said Lonergan, we must be self-aware and self-possessed. Thus, even this very philosophical study that creates an elaborate architecture of human knowing, at base wishes the human person to be whole in that understanding cannot be simply a matter of knowing facts and ordering them; it cannot be following directions or observing phenomena. Such an oddity as insight must be included in our dissection of how humans know. And the fact that it is a way of knowing means that we are creatures capable of thinking that is richer, deeper, and eminently more powerful than the "objective" means advocated for centuries by rationalists and empiricists.

Chapter 2 discusses more fully Lonergan's thoughts on the nature of insight. The most compelling of these and the one most necessary to cite here is the relation between the search for insight and our connection with others. Lonergan viewed the search for insight as containing the possibility of human growth. If we avoid or flee the conditions for insight, and those are dissonance and the confrontation of that dissonance, we risk isolation. For instance, when we refuse to grapple with a confounding situation, we can be gripped by it—whether it is a problem or a mystery—and we remain incapable of sharing ourselves (or isolated). In short, Lonergan would point us toward the examination of problems we face in order that we may grow internally and thus become rational and free—free to be responsible and act for the common good.

Insight and Rhetoric and Composition

Much of the efforts in the field of rhetoric and composition, in rediscovering the classical authors and in drawing from psychological theories of learning and development, lead to one desired end: an increase in the quality of thought in student writing. Considering how many writing-across-the-curriculum programs exist, these efforts have not been in vain. What writing promises to teachers and students ranges from increased recall (Emig, 1977; Langer & Applebee, 1987) to original synthesis of material (Lauer, 1982; Young, Becker, & Pike, 1970).

Every composition school encourages insight without knowing what it is. Expert writers Elbow (1973), Murray (1985), and Macrorie (1968) testified that writing surprises the writer with new meanings. Expressive writing enthusiasts believe that writing unlocks hidden thoughts. Both these groups encourage students to "wait" for the creative moment to occur. Elbow, for example, told students to create the environment in which these thoughts can occur. Some scholars such as Berthoff

(1981) or D'Angelo (1975) turn to psychological theories of hemisphericity or to an emphasis on the role of the imagination in writing. They tell students that if they only consult other parts of their brain, insights will occur. Education scholar Douglas Sloan (1983) also advocated use of the imagination to arrive at insight.

Flower and Hayes (1980), in their work with problem solving, debunk the "discovery" myth but still call writing a "meaning-making" activity. A final group of scholars draws from creativity theory in psychology, claiming that insight, as it is a component of creative acts, can appear in writing when writing is taught as a creative process (Gates, 1989; Lauer, 1967; Young et al., 1970). They tell students to walk through a series of heuristic procedures designed to encourage creativity and insight. Gates (1993) encouraged the use of insight and creativity as epistemological and pedagogical guides.

Variations of each of these approaches to insight in writing abound. Textbooks taut the terms *discovery* and *insight* for any prewriting activity. We are left to ponder what insight is, how to encourage it, and how to recognize it in developing papers.

Limitations and New Directions

If insight is contextually based, or produced, rather, in specific contexts, might it seem odd to question how researchers can let insight be insight and not restrict it by the goals of their research? In fact, each discipline does restrict or confine insight to the degree that it assigns a purpose to this mysterious event. No doubt insights do confer meaning, purpose, action, and peace, but they are larger in scope than the events they produce.

The questions that do not get asked best reveal the limitations and new directions for research. Probably the most important question that never gets asked is why insights, especially in popular understanding, are relegated to psychology when they are far-reaching and integrative events. The answer seems to be that insights, like love and religion, have been feminized, meaning they have been sequestered in the private world where they can do little harm to society at large. It is interesting to note, in comparison to Eastern notions, that our conception of insight is fragmented and controlled. Insights in our culture relate to specific events; we stop short often of applying them at a greater level. They are restricted to the understanding of maladaptive behavior patterns. In Eastern cultures, insight is a way of being.

The way insight is considered in our "modern Western

society" actually hinders adult development according to a number of thinkers today (see Hillman & Ventura, 1992; Miller, 1981; Schaef, 1992). Thomas Merton (1973), basing his work on Persian psychotherapist Reza Arasteh, explained that psychotherapy can keep society's most intelligent citizens from giving it pain. Arasteh combined his studies of Fromm, existential psychotherapy, and the logotherapy of Victor Frankl with Persian Sufism. Insight for Arasteh is health on a transcultural level:

> The man [sic] who has attained final integration is no longer limited by the culture in which he has grown up. "He has embraced *all of life*. . . . He has experienced qualities of every type of life": ordinary human existence, intellectual life, artistic creation, human love, religious life. He passes beyond all these limiting forms, while retaining all that is best and most universal in them, "finally giving birth to a fully comprehensive self." He accepts not only his own community, his own society, his own friends, his own culture, but all mankind. He does not remain bound to one limited set of values in such a way that he opposes them aggressively or defensively to others. He is fully "Catholic" in the best sense of the word. He has a unified vision and experience of the one truth shining out in all its various manifestations, some clearer than others, some more definite and more certain than others. He does not set these partial views up in opposition to each other, but unifies them in a dialectic or an insight of complementarity. With this view of life he is able to bring perspective, liberty and spontaneity into the lives of others. The finally integrated man is a peacemaker, and that is why there is such a desperate need for our leaders to become such men of insight. (p. 226)

To compare this description of insight with the typical rendition of psychological insight is to realize how limited our notions are.

The other question that is never asked is where the *content* of insights come from. Articles discuss whether insights are true or false, how a therapist can foster insight, and the qualities of insight, but no one discusses the content of the insight. By focusing on the hows, we ignore the sources of the wisdom we call insights. Social constructivists provide an answer. The content of an insight can be traced to the values that a person espouses, which social constructivists would say originate from communities of which the person is a part. In some cases, insights may be more relevatory of the communities we belong to rather than of the subject matter at hand. But even this answer is not enough, for we belong to many communities and choose values opposed to them at times.

Another question is why insights studied are largely verbal. A new direction for insight work is the study of how images lead to insight. Margaret Miles (1985) has developed an interesting approach. Exploring the territory of the child's inner world,renowned author Alice Miller (1981) claimed it was her experience of painting that led her to her very deep and important insights, not the years of training she had had in psychotherapy.

Finally, why is insight itself the focus, when the preparation for insight is equally important and valuable? Rainer Maria Rilke once wrote, and Joseph Campbell would agree, that it was important to live the questions rather than answer them. A focus on insight, especially on its qualities and aftereffects described after the fact, detracts from the powerful groundwork laid by awareness of dissonance and the ability to confront it.

Although much more study is needed of the event of insight, the experience itself (and the cultivation and hope for it) is a rich one for the individual and for society which makes it an important goal in college writing.

2

The 16 Features of Insight

A paradox exists when the construct of insight itself is addressed: Although great insights in all fields provide new perspectives and are, as such, of great importance, little is known about insight as a human phenomenon. Insight is also removed from common experience when considered a matter of genius or when restricted to therapy sessions; it is diluted when confined to matters of creativity. Because no field describes insight fully, an interdisciplinary approach is necessary. The most valid way to approach such a nebulous subject is to select only those features on which a number of scholars agree; that is what these 16 features represent.

Summary

The insight process, according to scholars in a variety of disciplines, is prefigured by dissonance, conscious or unconscious. No matter how surprising or spontaneous, the insight itself is the culmination of great inner pondering. It is the unconscious pondering of dissonance that makes insights appear without effort. Once a dissonance has been pondered (and well understood in its breadth), the individual confronts the dissonance. A complicated and often difficult process, confrontation often means the articulation of the unknown that the dissonance prompts us to resolve. To confront the dissonance with more than the intellect is another key to insight. Emotions, experiences, attitudes, and beliefs all play a part in confrontation.

Once an insight appears, it must be tested according to a number of criteria—experience, known solutions, and viability. The qualities of insight are most readily known: It is a radically new understanding or vision, typically simple and long-lasting in its truth. Insights help the knower differentiate between what is known and what is not known, providing a means to pursue further inquiry if necessary.

The aftereffects of insight make it a valuable pursuit for young scholars. Aside from peace at resolving a dissonance, individuals keep thinking about their insights, mining them for their richness. Action can be a likely result of insight now that direction is more apparent. It is not unusual that insights become part of the personal history of the knower and are employed in future situations.

College writers need the scholarly aspects of searching for insight: the cultivation and confrontation of complex and meaningful dissonances, shifts in perspective, and most especially the review of one's insights for continued scholarship.

PREREQUISITES OF INSIGHT

The prerequisites of insight, according to experts, are that one senses an incongruity and owns up to it. A student who cannot become curious about several readings in economics, for example, is not likely to produce an insight about them.

Dissonance

Dissonance refers to an incongruity a person experiences. Puzzlement, wonder, and curiosity all indicate dissonance, as do disappointment and suspicion. To be open to dissonance, and even to cultivate it, prepares one for insight. Even though popular understanding has insight seem effortless and spontaneous, the roots of insight lie in conscious or unconscious incongruity.

Unlike other types of learning or solutions to problems, insight, according to philosopher Lonergan (1957/1978), is "a function, not of outside forces, but of inner conditions" (p. 5). These inner conditions prepare individuals for insight. Theologian Shea (1980) also explained that what happens in revelation experiences is

> closely connected to what is happening in us before that experience. The needs that are troubling us, the drives that are urging us on, the conflicts that we are engaged in shape the content of the revelation. This does not mean that the revelation is caused by the needs, drives, or conflicts, but that they make us receptive, gear us to specific communications. (pp. 24-25)

Many theologians consider dissonance a precondition of revelation experiences. James (1902/1929) wrote that it is necessary for conversion; Batson, Ventis & Ventis (1982) called "uneasiness and solution" a characteristic of all religious experiences. Fawcett (1971) and theologians shaping what Dulles (1985) referred to as the "new awareness" model of revelation, all place dissonance at the beginning of the revelation experience. Implied in these considerations is that the lack of awareness (or worse, the silencing) of dissonance could theoretically prevent insight.

Psychologists Bruner (1963), Festinger (1957), and Piaget (1968) recognized in dissonance the beginning of learning. In accord with Lonergan and other theologians, they believe this inner instability begins a search that would never occur had it not been for the initial puzzlement. Piaget called the learning process "equilibrium" or the assimilation of the unknown into the known; Festinger, coining the term *cognitive dissonance*, like Bruner, wrote that inquiry takes place only after an incongruity is realized. Bruner believed that inquiry is the soundest base of education.

As composition theorists incorporate psychological theories into their descriptions of the writing process, they too see in writing the need for dissonance. Flower and Hayes (1980) described writing as an activity in which the active search for meaning is inherent. Lauer (1967) was the first to link writing to creativity, defining it as a creative process and thereby linking heuristic procedures (especially those concerning dissonance) to writing. Emig (1977) considered writing an activity wherein the writer can go beyond what is already known by engaging in the same learning process described by psychologists. Gates (1993) believed that insight and creativity need to be central aspects of epistemology and pedagogy in writing instruction.

Advocating dissonance as the beginning of inquiry, a variety of scholars encourage others to take up incongruities. Being permanently alert and attentive to the question, "Why," said Lonergan, begets the process of insight that leads to self-awareness and responsibility. The cultivation, recognition, and confrontation of dissonance "enhances the quality of [a student's] intellectual life" (p. xiv) according to Young, et al. (1970). They and Lauer, Montague, Emig, and Lunsford (1991) advised students to acknowledge "inconsistencies in [their] own image of the world" (p. 71) in order to develop academically and personally. Berthoff (1981) agreed that chaos has the potential to yield information when explored in detail (pp. 69-71).

The work of educator Paulo Freire (1982) illustrates how powerful education stemming from inquiry and the recognition of inconsistencies can be.

Confrontation

Confrontation is the most elusive and yet necessary part of the search for insight. Although the context of existential need or dissonance prepares us for inquiry, the action of confrontation itself does not necessarily follow. If the dissonance is unconscious (as many are), confrontation can accompany what Freud termed being able to "stomach" the subject matter. That is, confrontation is not simply the willingness to resolve a dissonance; because (and if) the dissonance often involves many aspects of the individual, that person must be ready, willing, and able to consider the complicated dissonance. The common image of a person having an insight while involved in physical activity unrelated to the dissonance points toward the unconscious aspect of confrontation as well. It also points to the need for a safe environment in which to consider dissonance and to the use of aspects of the individual beyond the intellect at a time when the intellect is not dominant.

Scholars in a number of fields concur that no confrontation means no insight. Labov and Fanshel (1977) saw this relationship in their work on analyzing therapeutic discourse. In a 10-year case study, the patient could not confront the dissonance she felt and never produced an insight. Lonergan believes the flight from insight or lack of confrontation "generates misunderstanding both in ourselves and in others": If we let fantasies or old ways of understanding overrule the possibility of attaining new insights, especially from consulting with others, we risk the lack of human development (p. 191).

Confronting dissonance can and often does mean facing that which is nebulous, troublesome, complex, and even wordless. Thus, some scholars refer to the activity of confrontation as one of questioning. It becomes the articulation of the unknown. Theologians see this moment of wondering as the opportunity for understanding the larger context of one's life through understanding specific issues. Tillich (1951) wrote that revelation is never abstract; Dulles (1985) explained that it is "always correlated with human questions arising out of a specific cultural and historical context" (p. 102). Psychologists Mathieu-Coughlan and Klein (1984) related that a driving, questioning attitude along with "focusing" will lead patients to higher levels of integration of their feelings and thoughts. This integration of feeling and thought—according to Waskow and Parloff (1975), authors of *Psychotherapy Change Measures*, a commentary on psychological tests—corresponds highly to the construct of insight.

Guidance for confrontation is included in the composition pedagogies of Lauer et al. (1991); Young et al. (1970); and Berthoff (1981). Asking students to acknowledge, articulate, and explore dissonances enforces confrontation. Lauer et al. asked students to form a question that points them toward the unknown that they must investigate. Young et al. have students state the dissonance as a problem. Berthoff asked students to explore chaos in a dialectical fashion. Many composition texts include prewriting activities that seem to foster confrontation; however if the activity is only brainstorming on a topic and not on a specific question, confrontation is not fostered. The difference, experts agree, may mean the difference between exposition and unique understandings.

Although difficult and elusive, the skill of confrontation of dissonance is a key to the readiness for insight.

QUALITIES OF INSIGHT

Once a person acknowledges and confronts a dissonance, a search for a solution begins. No one understands the exact ways insights come about, thus the qualities described are those seen in retrospect.

New Understanding

It is the novelty of insights that make them so compelling. An insight exists on another plane than typical or various solutions to a dissonance—that is why they are novel.

Several scholars claimed insights show us patterns. Snyder (1945) defined insight as such; Shea (1980) and Baum (1973) believe insight is the perception of life-giving "patterns in human existence"; Lonergan (1957/1978) said that even the perception that there is no pattern to a certain dissonance is in itself an insight—an "inverse" one. Elbow (1973) said that while writing one can see "a shape where a moment ago there was none" (p. 35). The pattern is the resolution of the various facets of dissonance that once caused wonder.

The novelty of insights can perhaps be explained by the requirement, as many writers show, of an entirely new mindset toward the problem. Dulles (1985) expressed it best as "a breakthrough to a higher level of consciousness as humanity is drawn to a fuller participation in the divine creativity" (p. 115). Rahner (1966) described revelatory events, according to Dulles, as "a new mode of human consciousness in which the human spirit perceives itself as finalized toward the divine in a new way, and perceives the divine as drawing the human spirit into closer union with itself" (p. 100). Baum (1973) referred to this new understanding of revelation as "new awareness" and "salvational truth . . . [that] raises man's consciousness" (p. 16). Such is the paradox of insight, however, that it brings new consciousness without our knowing how it did so.

Many composition theorists consider writing to be capable of attaining a new mindset. Writing can portray dissonance (as do many other art forms) in movable symbols (words); in manipulating symbols a writer can more easily reach a resolution (Young et al. 1970). Several composition theorists have students echo the creative process outlined by Wallas (1926) in order to make insight or illumination the goal of writing (Gates, 1993; Lauer et al., 1991; Young et al., 1970).

Expert writers testify to the possibility writing holds for new understanding. Murray (1985) believes "writing tells its own story" and discussed the power writing has to surprise the writer. Elbow (1986) said that insights resulting from creative and intuitive writing exercises (without care for form and style) are "fresh" and "not connected to prejudice, stock responses, or the desire for consistency" (p. 56).

New Vision

When discussing insight, many writers use a visual metaphor. This metaphor is used so often that to omit it would be to rob the construct of one of its most constant descriptors.

Schafer (1978) coined an expression that best expresses this feature: Insight is "a way of looking." Mahrer (1985) further explained that insight "indicates a substantial change in the way the patient sees himself and his world" (p. 118). Ohlsson (1984) applied the problem-solving literature to insight, stating that "insight occurs when a representation change brings the goal state within the horizon of mental look-ahead" (p. 124). These psychologists equated change in vision with change in understanding.

James (1929) also used the visual metaphor to explain religious experiences. He wrote that people reporting religious experiences testify to an "objective change which the world often appears to undergo" (p. 243). Baum (1973) echoed the psychologists in writing that "revelation constitutes a new awareness in man through which he sees the world in a new light. . ." (p. 16). The word *insight* itself contains the visual term *sight*. The grasping of something new may require something of our visual capacities even though we do not know how the mind works. If, as some scholars suggest, the mind works in images, this metaphor may not be metaphor at all.

Simple Solution

Insights are simple and elegant. Klein et al. (1969) believe that the person with insight is capable of "reducing/reintegrating . . . solutions to a more basic principle" (p. 63). Labov and Fanshel (1977), a linguist and a psychologist respectively, also described insight as a basic principle. Using the speech act theory of Searle (1969), they developed a description of therapeutic discourse wherein they characterized insight as a proposition. In other words, insight is a truth-telling statement, one in which the speaker articulates some knowledge he or she has reached.

The best word used to describe this process of coming to a simple solution is that of Shea (1970): He wrote that people "distill" the revelation-faith experience until they create a "a proverb, slogan, or one-line truism" (p. 23). Lonergan (1957/1978) may have summarized these thoughts on the simplicity of insights when he said "every insight unifies and organizes" (p. xii).

Permanently True

An added benefit to insights, along with their simplicity, is that they last.

Lonergan believed that insights are not subject to revision, unlike empirical knowledge which can be reinterpreted using the data which it is founded (pp. 335-336). Rahner (1966) believes that because insights are founded on "the transcendental and the predicamental" they are expressed "in conceptual language having a permanently valid content" (p. 101). Psychologists during the 1960s and 1970s were concerned with the truth value of an insight; they concluded that only those insights that patients acted on were true (Schafer, 1978; Segal, 1962; Shonbar, 1965).

The experience of having a series or number of insights might seem to contradict the belief that insights are permanently true. Certainly in a psychological sense, insights range in their depth. What Lonergan and Rahner referred to is the fullness of experience in having an insight. Limiting either the sense of self or of the information needed can restrict the depth of the dissonance and therefore of the insight.

Whole Person

Until dissonance is approached with the whole self—mind, heart, behavior—headaches rather than solutions are likely to result. Shea (1980), a theologian (and sometime poet and storyteller), best explained this most agreed upon feature:

> The phrase "faith-formulation" can give the mistaken impression that responses to a revelatory event are primarily intellectual efforts. And in the history of the theology of revelation and faith the cognitive value of these experiences has been heavily stressed. But the revelation-faith experience itself engulfs the whole person. They affect the centered self, addressing the mind, heart and behavior. (p. 24)

American pragmatist philosopher Fontinell (1970) believed revelation to be "essentially noncognitive" and linked it to symbolic language as does Rahner. O'Meara (1975) quoted Rahner who considered revelation a "state of mind—not knowledge but a consciousness" (p. 415). Intellectual efforts at solving problems prove futile according to psychologists as well.

When psychologists hold that catharsis, or emotional release, signals insight, they too note the involvement of the whole self. Brady (1967) wrote that "to be meaningful, the qualifying term emotional must denote insight accompanied by the perception and expression of appropriate affective change" (p. 305). Brady (1967) and London (1964) referred to insight with an emotional release as a *true* insight; the release is a sort of verification of the insight's correctness as well as an indication of how relevant the solution is to the patient's life. True or emotional insights are believed to effect lasting behavior changes. In contrast, insights of purely intellectual nature—missing the emotional response—are termed *false* or *temporary* (Bandura, 1965; Brady, 1967; London, 1964). These insights are believed not to yield lasting behavior change. Another psychologist interested in charting "indices of movement," suggested that insights that are "meaningful, significant, and therapeutically important" are "accompanied by emotional arousal" (Mahrer, 1985, p. 118).

Several psychologists wrote that insight integrates the cognitive and affective domains of a person. Schafer (1978) said that for the patient with true insight "the past and present are considerably more extensive, cohesive, consistent, humane, and convincingly felt than they were before" (p. 18). The emphasis here is on the word "felt"; however, the integration of past and present experiences is also important. He added "they are more intelligible and tolerable even if still not very enjoyable or tranquil" (p. 18). In other words, the person has an intellectual understanding and an emotional grip on the situation simultaneously. The person has integrated emotions with understanding.

Several experts make the integration of emotion and cognition their definition of insight. Klein et al. (1969) designed an experiencing scale, the highest level of which describes the patient being able to give a "full, easy presentation of experiencing" in which "all elements are confidently integrated" (p. 64). Labov and Fanshel (1977) similarly defined *insight* as the patient's ability to be in touch with his or her feelings (p. 54). Two prominent researchers in insight studies, Strupp and Binder (1984), defined *insight* as "affective experiencing and cognitive understanding of current maladaptive patterns of behavior that repeat childhood patterns of interpersonal conflict" (pp. 24-25).

Berthoff (1981) and Elbow (1981) encouraged students to use their imagination, particularly in affective ways, to achieve insights. Elbow, at one point, even advised students to write lies simply because they break the traditional cognitive approach to problems. Lauer et al. incorporated the affective dimension in the exploration of dissonance: Students write out their attitudes toward their subject alongside facts they remember.

Limits of Knowledge

Insight, as Lonergan said, is knowledge of knowledge. The dissonance confronted earlier is now seen in perspective. The insight
acts like a lamp that discloses where we are, where we were, and
where we have to go.

Shengold (1981) believes that insight reveals our intellectual boundaries. He said, "we should know the limits of what
we know and what we don't know, both as to contents and qualities
of our knowing" (p. 293). Tillich (1951) offered much the same
view. Baltazar (1966) interpreted revelation for Tillich to be an
event that "increases the dim light of reason so that it can see the
depths of the future and know where to go to attain its goal" (p.
177). Insight, for Teilhard de Chardin, according to Baltazar, is
"is immutable—not as an idea, not as a content, but as a direction" (p. 177).

Because revelation-faith experiences, according to Shea
(1980), place our actions within a larger context, they can be
shocking. They are a recognition of the "wrongheadedness" of a
life that has "so gone against the grain of the Mystery within
which it lives" (p. 26). Weiner (1975) and Strupp and Binder
(1984) also considered the recognition of poor behavior patterns
as a kind of exposure of the limits of knowledge. Previous ways of
acting become the subject for intellectual activity.

VERIFICATION

The term *insight* frequently refers to any sudden flash of meaning
or quick solution. Experts distinguish among insights, as it were,
by their veracity and staying power. Insights should resolve dissonance simply and completely. Before insights are employed,
they are tested, because not every quick idea does in fact resolve
dissonance. Young et al. cautioned that:

> the intellectual explorer must be willing to accept risks and
> the failures that so often accompany exploration. Hard
> work, false starts, and inadequate hypotheses seem to be
> preconditions for successful innovation; they are normal,
> perhaps necessary, features of innovative thought and
> should be accepted as such. (p. 135)

Scholars suggest two methods of verifying insights: living them out and thinking them through. Freud said that insights had to be "worked through" before they could be considered true. Shea (1980) affirmed Freud and other psychologists when he wrote that revelation-faith experiences are "mobilized and tested in the real world" (p. 24). The person "purges" the new revelation by living out the meaning. Young et al. (1970) concurred that actual use of the insight will help verify it.

Another tack is logical thinking. Perkins (1981) said even great ideas and artistic creations may still have flaws that need attention. He suggested employing judgment to detect them (p. 127). In his book, *Embracing Contraries*, Elbow (1986) advised writers to employ logical or critical thinking after producing ideas freely. In this way, writers embrace contrary types of thinking: Intuitive and creative thinking should espouse logical and critical appraisal (p. 60). Young et al. (1970) also suggested comparing the insight with experience and with reliable knowledge established over time (p. 156). Westerman (1989) qualified his position by insisting that insights need to relate to clients' meaningful activities; that is, he believes that insights have to be rooted in action, but in meaningful action.

EFFECTS OF INSIGHT

Composition teachers employ all of the previously discussed features to encourage thoughtful writing; however, these next features are the fruits of their labor almost always gone unseen. They sometimes appear in student work, but more frequently blossom over time. It is only when, at a future date, students return to share their experiences that teachers catch a glimpse of the power of insights.

Action

Imagine a student in a political science class who resolved a complex dissonance that arose from a variety of readings. That student may be found not only discussing his or her ideas, but implementing them somewhere if an insight has occurred.

A feature of action encompasses the enactment of the idea and commitment to it. In his description of the faith-formulation process, Shea (1980) gave a "pride of place" to action:

In a similar way the faith-formulation process is an activity of the whole person, unfolding the convictions, feelings and behaviors which are suggested in the experience. At any given time the mind or heart or the need to embody the meaning in action will play the dominant role. But all are always present and operative. However, a certain "pride of place" must be given to action. In action the convictions and feelings are mobilized and tested in the real world. It is in living out the project hidden in the revelation-faith experience that we extend and own, deepen and purge that experience. The last moment of the faith-formulation process is the businessman, the college girl, and the son engaged in a new way in an old world. (p. 24)

Change in lifestyle is what James (1902/1929) also considered a product of personal revelation (p. 243). Lonergan (1957/1978) wrote: "man's explanatory self-knowledge can become effective in his concrete living only if the content of systematic insights, the direction of judgments, the dynamism of decisions can be embodied in images that release feeling and emotion and flow spontaneously into deeds no less than words" (p. 547).

Psychologists have traditionally assumed that action follows insight. The 1960s and 1970s saw psychologists referring to insights with action as "true" (Fenishel, 1945) and those without as "false" (Bandura, 1961; Brady, 1967; London, 1964). Contemporary psychologists (Blum, 1979; Neubauer, 1979; Wallerstein, 1983), however, hold up an awesome challenge: the explanation of change without insight and insight without change, both of which occur. Neubauer wrote: "the relative paucity of papers on the subject of insight indicates that we take its role for granted and have not bothered to explore fully the relation of insight and clinical improvement" (p. 30). Even so, many psychologists would hold with Mahrer (1985) that insight has "significant implications for the patient's well-being and personal and interpersonal behavior" (p. 118).

Committed action is what Baum (1973) and Dulles (1985) described as resulting from insight. Baum wrote that the revelation experience "constitutes a new awareness in man through which he sees the world in a new light and commits himself to a new kind of action" (p. 16). Dulles saw in the new awareness model of revelation a "commitment to peace [and] justice. . . ." (p. 122).

Peace

An overriding, perhaps obvious, characteristic of insight that is not written about much is the peace or relief that it brings.

"Loss of worry," as James wrote is how most writers characterize this feature. Psychologists such as Mendel (1975) stated that once "meaning is assigned" four effects are present: Anxiety lessens, repression is lifted (more material available in memory), subjective relief is felt from a variety of symptoms, and dreams shed light on issues resolved by the assignment of meaning (p. 410). Much of the material on catharsis connected with insight in the dimension of the whole person is relevant here also in that the emotional release signals the relief mentioned by Mendel.

Expansive Understanding

A solution to a problem, like finding the call number of a library book, can be quickly forgotten once the task is completed. Insights, however, are not forgotten. Another quality of insights is that their meanings are pondered long after the insight event.

Despite the sudden appearance of most insights, wrote Shea (1980), their "appropriation is usually slow. Revelation-faith experiences carry with them a sense of 'too much' and 'very important.' The result is that the events are remembered, rehashed, and slowly, meanings are clarified. The metaphors for this process are: mining the richness, surfacing the depth, unpacking what is compressed" (p. 23). When they describe the revelation experience as one of consciousness raising, Dulles, Rahner, and Baum implied that the experience causes more reflection on the experience. As Shea said, these experiences are "open-ended and ongoing" (p. 23).

Klein et al. (1969) have heard patients with insight integrate thought and emotion in an "expansive, unfolding" and even "buoyant" way. Lonergan wrote that "homogeneous expansion" occurs after insight; that is, from the original insight more and richer information comes without change or nullification of the original insight (p. 15).

Part of Personal History

Insights become part of our personal history; that is, we own them in a personal way once we reduce the experience to a portable form.

Mendel (1975), a psychologist, wrote that insights become "part of the lifestyle, history and future way" of understanding things (p. 411). Lonergan believed that "insight passes into the habitual texture of one's mind" (p. 6). Unless this ownership occurs, wrote Weiner (1975), behavior change cannot occur.

Portability aids ownership. Klein et al. described insight-possessing individuals as capable of "reducing/reintegrating solutions to a more basic solution" that then becomes portable, as Weiner described it. Shea (1980) described this phenomenon in terms of a maxim. He wrote:

> This meaning, now detached from life-giving dialogue with the experience, accompanies the person through life. It often takes the form of a proverb, slogan, or one-line truism. The businessman will say at a cocktail party, "You've got to get to know your grandchildren." The college girl will judge future acquaintances in terms of their self-centeredness. The son will say, "When it's your time, it's your time. You have to go with it." While these crystallized life-learnings can be communicated to others, they often appear arbitrary. Finalized faith-formulations make the most sense when they are related to the whole process which preceded them. (pp. 23-24)

Interpreting Device

That "more basic principle" or "maxim" that experts wrote of to describe insight as a part of a person's personal history is used as an interpreting device for past, present, and future events.

Mendel wrote that once the insight has become "part of the lifestyle" it is used to interpret things and events (p. 411). Once patients have formed a "basic principle," according to Klein et al., they apply "general principles to a range of situations" (p. 63). Shea wrote that "revelation is often described as an event which makes other events intelligible. . . . The event does not make other events intelligible; but we who have received a meaning through the event try to bring other events within its sphere of influence without jeopardizing their integrity" (p. 50). In another place, Shea referred to revelation-faith experiences as "life orientations" that "do not produce 'how to' hints but fundamental perspectives and attitudes" (p. 32).

FACILITATORS

Because the experience of insight can neither be predicted nor summoned, no specific pathway toward insight is addressed; nevertheless, shifting perspectives and providing a welcoming atmosphere seem to encourage insight.

Perspective Shift

Creativity scholars point toward the conscious development of novel associations. Noy (1978) advised creating connections between thought and emotion, emotion and motivation, between isolated thoughts, and between linear and nonlinear thoughts. He also suggested assigning new contexts to what is learned in other contexts. DeBono (1970, 1992), Guilford (1967), and Rothenberg (1979) also testified to the need to create new associations. Perkins (1981), like Noy, offered a wide array of activities, including planning, abstracting, undoing, and making means into ends. Lonergan (1957/1978) also noted the importance of linking the unlikely as "insight pivots between the concrete and abstract" (p. 5).

Elliott, James, Reimschuessel, Cislo, and Sack (1985) described perspective shift as the most "helpful" event in a therapy session. Their analysis is discussed in terms of clusters; they described the "new perspective" cluster as including "the psychodynamic notion of insight (Roback, 1974; Weiner, 1975) as well as the contemporary notion of cognitive restructuring (e.g., Beck, Rush, Shaw, & Emery, 1979; Meichenbaum, 1977)" (p. 318).

Theologians also share the belief that insight involves a shift in perspective. Dulles wrote that revelation "contributes to the restructuring of experience and the transformation of the self and the world" (p. 109). Shea wrote that revelation experiences "provide a particularly powerful illumination of our relationships to Mystery" (p. 33).

Lunsford, a writing specialist, (1980) noted a special need for perspective shift: Basic writers "merge with the topic; they cannot distance themselves in order to gain a variety of perspectives on the topic" (p. 281). Flower and Hayes (1980) and Perl (1978) agreed that students often lack unique and developed problem representation. Young et al. (1970) offered the tagmemic heuristic as an aid to seeing multiple perspectives. In *Embracing Contraries,* Elbow (1986) suggested embracing con-

trary types of thinking: intuitive, creative thinking and later logical, critical thinking (p. 56). Berthoff (1981) stated that
meaning is made from a dialectical process determined by perspective and context.

Of course, shifting perspectives does not imply instant
insights. Unless the preconditions of dissonance and confrontation
exist, insights are not likely to occur. A means of encouraging
writers to shift perspective is to encourage intuitive and emotional responses that have no rational foundations. Pursuing such
responses, as Belenky et al. (1986), the writers of *Women's
Ways of Knowing* attest, leads to an integrated understanding.

Welcoming Atmosphere

Another facilitator of insight is a welcoming atmosphere. Insights
do not occur when, in therapy, a client is neither accepted nor
welcomed. Snyder (1945) and Elliott (1985) found that what
was most frustrating or hindering in therapy was being misun-
derstood.

Mathieu-Coughlan and Klein (1984) advised therapists to
affirm the experiences of clients, to steer them toward the integration of thought emotion and common perceptions, and to provide the accepting atmosphere that would allow the integration
full room to take place. The familiar experience of solving a
problem while engaging in manual activity might be evidence for a
safe or welcoming place as well. When the intellect is not in full
force, other aspects of the person can come forth.

The work of Freire (1982) has influenced composition
teachers regarding the creation of a welcoming atmosphere in the
classroom. Fostering intellectual growth using invention heuris-
tics from psychology and classical rhetoric has forced composition
teachers to abandon their authoritarian stance as teachers.

CONCLUSION

This chapter has identified 16 dimensions of insight as described by
scholars from a variety of fields. I have categorized the features
into prerequisites: dissonance, confrontation; qualities: new understanding, new vision, simple solution, permanently true, involvement of the whole self, exposes the limits of knowledge; verification: needs testing; effects: action, peace, expansive understanding,

becomes part of personal history, used as interpreting device; and facilitators: perspective shift, and welcoming atmosphere.

Table 2.1 displays the great similarity in descriptions of insight offered by psychologists, theologians, and the philosopher Lonergan. Composition theorists do not share the same breadth of features for several reasons. If students have an insight while writing one assignment, the effects of that insight are usually not the subject for the next assignment, which most typically concerns another subject entirely. Finally, the communication setting is not as firm as those available to psychologists and theologians. Students and teachers may take leave of each other's company too soon thus preventing further discussion of their writing. Chapter 3 demonstrates how teachers and researchers can identify insight in student texts.

Table 2.1. Convergence of Descriptions of Insight

Dimension	Psychology	Theology/Philosophy	Composition
Prerequisites			
Dissonance	X	X	X
Confrontation	X	X	X
Qualities			
New understanding	X	X	X
New vision	X	X	X
Simple solution	X	X	
Permanently true	X	X	
Whole person	X	X	X
Limits of knowledge	X	X	
Verification			
Needs testing	X	X	X
Effects			
Action	X	X	
Peace	X	X	
Expansive			

Table 2.1. Convergence of Descriptions of Insight (cont.)

understanding	X	X	
Part of personal history	X	X	
Interpreting device	X	X	
Facilitators			
Perspective shift	X	X	X
Welcoming atmosphere	X	X	X

3

A Textual Scale
for Insight

The preceding chapter concerning the dimensions of insight may have triggered memories of essays of former students or of conversations held with authors. Maybe Sarah achieved peace at the close of an essay; Juan may refer to the discovery he made in office conferences; maybe Leticia now understands the intellectual boundaries that she must transcend in order to solve her puzzlement. But this collection of descriptions, although thought-provoking, will not enable teachers to identify insight in student writing for a number of reasons.

Sixteen dimensions are too cumbersome, and how many of them qualify an essay as insightful? Even more important, insight is not always expressed as such in student writing. In fact, glimpses of it can appear rather than a full expression of insight. Although the 16 categories are interesting, they need to be organized in a more manageable form. They also need to be keyed to student writing. Writing teachers need to be able to see the dimensions as manifested by students who are not always in control of either their thinking or their writing.

This chapter presents a review of attempts to measure insight, and includes a measure for insight in student writing, and a brief discussion of its development.

MEASURING INSIGHT: A REVIEW OF THE LITERATURE

Measuring anything requires two activities: defining and counting. Measurement experts refer to an operational definition as one that allows them to both define and count. When a construct, such as height or weight, is easily counted, the operational definition comes very close to the exact construct. When the construct is more abstract, like leadership, for example, the operational definition provides outward indicators to use in labeling a phenomenon. The operational definition of leadership might include a count of the number of positions a person holds in social organizations. The next section discusses psychologists' work in operationally defining and measuring the construct of insight.

Insight Measures

Psychologists have developed several measures to analyze the client-therapist dialogue in order to determine whether insight is reached. Most of the research relies on transcripts of the conversation, but in one study a videotape of the session was used to identify the insight. The following measures are discussed in terms of their definitions of insight, of the unit they analyze, and of their validity and reliability.

In 1945, Snyder developed an *Insight Measure* (see Table 3.1), defining insight as the ability to see patterns and relationships that indicate "logical and reasoned explanations rather than a rationalization" (p. 200). He coded more than 10,000 responses, using as a unit of analysis a statement of understanding or insight. He considered a "break in ideas" a text boundary. No validity figures are reported although Snyder did have an "untrained" and "disinterested" rater recheck some of his work to verify his categories. Reliability figures range from .76 to .87 using the test-retest method on his own scoring. Snyder stated that the task was too large to use another rater.

Table 3.1. Snyder's (1945) Insight Measure

YUI		where YUI=understanding
--------------	x 100	or insight
YUI + YSP		YSP=problem
		statements

Over an 8-year period, Klein, Mathieu, Gendlin, and Kiesler (1969) developed the *Experiencing Scale* from the work of Carl Rogers who drew from Eugene Gendlin. They defined experiencing as "the quality of an individual's experiencing of himself, the extent to which his ongoing, bodily, felt flow of experiencing is the basic datum of his awareness and communications about himself, and the extent to which this inner datum is integral to action and thought" (p. 1).

They used as a unit of analysis the subjects in the patient's speech, derived optimally from 5- to 8-minute therapy sessions. Their measure (see Table 3.2) is a 7-point annotated and anchored scale, ranging from discussion of external events (Stage 1) to "full, easy presentation of experiencing" in which "all elements are confidently integrated" (Stage 7) (p. 64).

Klein et al. noted that content validity for the scale comes from Gendlin's success in reworking the definition of experiencing from a notion of a "storehouse of events" to a notion of "dynamic process" as the "basic felt datum or referent of awareness that changes from poorer, more vague, more rigid, to richer, more concrete, more confident, that is, a shift from incongruent to congruent" (p. 3).

Stage 7, in their measure, most closely corresponds to the construct of insight defined here. Descriptions of the self are "applied to an expanding range of inner events or give rise to new insights" (p. 63). Four conditions illustrate this development:

1. exploring an inner problem, and applying the conclusion to other problems;
2. reintegrating previous solutions, more developed synthesis;
3. reducing/reintegrating of solutions to a more basic principle; and
4. application of general principles to a range of situations (p. 63).

This instrument includes several features of insight discussed in Chapter 2. Klein et al. defined Stage 7 as "expansive, unfolding." The client is "euphoric, buoyant, confident . . . [conveys] a sense of things falling quickly and meaningfully into place" (p. 63). Their description mentions a sense of peace and satisfaction at resolving a dissonance. They achieved very high reliability on their measure for both clinically sophisticated and unsophisticated raters: both scored over .90 (p. 39).

Table 3.2. The Experiencing Scale (Klein et al., 1969)

Stage	Content	Treatment
1	External events; refusal to participate	Impersonal, detached
2	External events; behavioral or intellectual self-description	Interested, personal, self-participation
3	Personal reactions to external events; limited self-description; behavioral descriptions of feelings	Reactive, emotionally involved
4	Descriptions of feelings and personal experiences	Self-descriptive, associative
5	Problems or propositions about feelings and personal experiences	Exploratory, elaborative, hypothetical
6	Direct sense of emergent feelings and their impact affirmative	Feelings vividly expressed, spontaneous or
7	Easy presentation of experiencing; elements confidently integrated	Expansive, illuminating, confident, buoyant

Note. Copyright ©1970 by M. Klein. Revised, 1983. Reprinted with permission of the author.

Waskow and Parloff (1975), editors of *Psychotherapy Change Measures*, consider the Experiencing Scale the closest measure of the construct of insight but stated that "perhaps there is no one measure of insight or experiencing that sensitively reflects change for the `patients' in psychotherapy" (p. 100).

In 1985, Elliott used a videotape to begin to identify the most helpful events in psychoanalysis. Using Kagan's (1975) Interpersonal Process Recall method of tape-assisted recall, he asked three people—the client, the therapist, and an observer—to isolate helpful events on a videotape of a therapy session. Having identified helpful events, Elliott (1985) performed two cluster analyses on remarks about these helpful events. One cluster that emerged was the "new perspective," which included insight. He explained that "the hallmark of the new perspective events was the counselor's providing the student with some form of new information, resulting in increased insight, awareness, or cognitive restructuring" (p. 311). He considered the new perspective cluster to include "the psychodynamic notion of insight (Roback, 1974; Weiner, 1975), as well as the contemporary notion of cognitive restructuring (e.g., Beck, Rush, Shaw, & Emery, 1979; Meichenbaum, 1977)" (p. 318).

In a second cluster analysis (Elliott, James, Reimschuessel, Cislo, & Sack, 1985), the new perspective cluster was split into personal insight and interpersonal insight by means of content analysis. Based on this work, Elliott created a measure called a Therapeutic Impact Content Analysis System that includes operational definitions of personal and impersonal insights (Table 3.3). He operationally defined personal insight as "realizing something new about self, including gaining cognitive insight, seeing new connections about self or about self in relationship to others" (p. 622). He discussed impersonal insight, a rare occurrence, as "new information about third parties or people in general" (p. 623). He discussed validity in terms of the similarity of these findings to "central theoretical constructs in the major theories of psychotherapy: Insight . . . correspond[s] to the psychoanalytic concept of insight, working through. . . (Weiner, 1975)" (p. 628). Reliability for this measure was .69 (Cronbach's alpha) for four raters identifying insight in 93 cases.

No one study of insight could be more disappointing than that of Labov and Fanshel (1977), and certainly not because of the lack of quality. The famous linguist Labov and psychologist Fanshel studied therapeutic discourse for 10 years using one case study. They operationally defined insight as the patient's ability to

Table 3.3. Therapeutic Impact Content Analysis System: Abbreviated Definitions and Examples (Elliott et al., 1985)

I. Helpful Impacts

A. Task Impacts: Client describes progress toward completion of tasks of therapy.

1. Personal Insight: Client describes realizing something new about self, including gaining cognitive insight, seeing new connections about self or about self in relationship to others.
   Example: It did make me realize something about myself that I hadn't thought about.

2. Awareness: Client describes approaching uncomfortable experiences, including lessening or overcoming blocks to experiencing of uncomfortable thoughts, feelings, perceptions.
   Example: T helped me bring out an emotion that I hadn't really wanted to look at before.

3. Clarification of Problem: Client describes becoming clearer about the definition of his or her problems, tasks, or goals for therapy.
   Example: That helped me to get a better understanding of what I'm going to have to work on in therapy.

4. Problem Solution: Client describes progress toward plan of action, including specification of alternatives, selection of a course of action, or learning how to cope with situations outside of therapy.
   Example: It allowed me to figure out what I should do about my problem, and what wouldn't work.

B. Interpersonal Impacts: Client describes helpful interpersonal contact with therapist.

5. Understanding: Client describes being accurately or deeply understood by the therapist, especially in relation to the client's experiences or person.
   Example: I felt T really saw how I felt.

6. Reassurance: Client describes experiencing either a sense of relief from painful feelings, such as guilt, or the enhancement of positive feelings, such as self-worth, self-confidence, or general hopefulness.
   Example: I felt more confident that I could control my problem.

7. Involvement: Client describes being cognitively stimu-

Table 3.3. Therapeutic Impact Content Analysis System: Abbreviated Definitions and Examples (Elliott et al., 1985) (cont.)

---

lated or working harder or becoming more involved or invested in the tasks of therapy.
Example: It started me thinking and I felt better about where therapy was going.

8. Personal Contact: Client describes experiencing a greater sense of therapist as a person or fellow human being. Includes perception of positive characteristics of therapist as a person and the experience of mutuality or sharing activities with the therapist.
Example: He showed he had my best interests in mind.

II. Hindering Impacts:

9. Unwanted Thoughts: Client describes feeling discomfort resulting from being forced or stimulated to confront unpleasant experiences, facts, or memories. May include increasing avoidance or warding off, tighter self-control, or greater defensiveness.
Example: It was bothersome again. I had to think about it again. It made me want to not think about it all, the whole situation.

10. Unwanted Responsibility: Client describes feeling disappointed or pressured by having all or most of the responsibility for change placed on him or her.
Example: T's response put pressure on me to think of something to talk about next.

11. Misperception: Client describes therapist as misunderstanding, having missed the point of what the client is saying, or using the wrong words.
Example: I felt that maybe T wasn't understanding me. I didn't know how far back, but I felt that T was confused at what I was saying.

12. Negative Therapist Reaction: Client describes therapist as responding negatively to client, as being either uninvolved, inattentive or self-indulgent; or attacking or critical.
Example: I hardly ever talk about that really personal stuff, and she didn't seem to care.

13. Misdirection: Client describes therapist as interrupting, confusing, or sidetracking the client's exploration or interfering with the client's chosen focus.

Table 3.3. Therapeutic Impact Content Analysis System: Abbreviated Definitions and Examples (Elliott et al., 1985) (cont.)

Example: It was an interruption to what I was saying and thinking about. I didn't want to break the flow.

14. Repetition: Client describes becoming impatient, bored, or critical of therapist because therapist's responses are trivial, repeat already-covered material, or are leading nowhere.
Example: I thought that was already taken care of; we had already gotten out of that and it was sort of irrelevant to go back to it.

III. Other Impacts

15. Other. This scale includes less frequent types of impact: (a) interpersonal insight (i.e., new information about third parties or people in general); (b) demoralization; (c) impacts not elsewhere described; and (d) unscorable (i.e., events that contain no scorable impacts).

Ratings are based on manifest content, using the following scale: 0—*Clearly absent.* 1—*Slight evidence for presence, or inferred from content but not stated directly.* 2—*Probably present but not sure, or clearly present, but only mentioned.* 3—*Clearly present and elaborated.* For complete definitions and examples, see Elliott et al., (1984). Permission to reprint granted by the author.

be in touch with his or her feelings (p. 54). Using speech act theory (Searle, 1969), they gave insight propositional status and wished to isolate recurrent messages to build a theory of therapeutic discourse. Unfortunately, however, the patient never had an insight.

In summary, the insight measures presented were four: Snyder's Insight Measure, Klein et al.'s Experiencing Scale, Elliott's Therapeutic Impact Content Analysis System, and Labov and Fanshel's linguistic analysis. The work of Klein et al. and Elliott show that insight can be reliably and validly measured, providing examples of how insight can be measured in writing.

In psychology, Roback (1974) and Wallerstein (1983) related how nebulous the term *insight* has been. Common notions of insight discussed by Perkins (1981) are that insight is abstract, comes from out of the blue, requires genius or special thought processes, and is irregular in occurrence. The tests just discussed, however, challenge common notions of insight. As they show, insight can be reliably recognized in videotapes of therapy sessions and in the client-therapist dialogue. Can it be measured in student writing however?

CRITERIA FOR A MEASURE OF INSIGHT IN COMPOSITION

Two of the four tests discussed in the previous section are reliable and valid. This section describes why these tests cannot be applied to composition and why a new test must be developed.

Of the four tests reviewed, Klein et al.'s Experiencing Scale looks the most adaptable to composition research, but it poses two problems. This scale analyzes the client-therapist dialogue for integration of thought and emotion; as such, the dialogue is an appropriate subject to analyze because therapists elicit patients' feelings. Expressive writing, however, will not manifest insight as a result of dialogue. Moreover, it will express insight using any number of organizational schemes and in any variety of degrees. That is, students can elect to share any amount of insight they wish and organize the essay in ways that may veil it from the reader (although in essence expressive writing offers the greatest opportunity for the visible manifestation of insight). Therefore, Klein et al.'s scale is not the appropriate medium for research in writing. Second, the scale may miss certain elements of insight that do not conform to the direct statement of integration of thought and emotion. The construct of insight as described in the literatures discussed in Chapter 2 contains more dimensions than are described in the Experiencing Scale.

Elliott's Therapeutic Impact Content Analysis System cannot be considered a viable measure for composition research because it is tied too closely to the therapy session. Unlike the Experiencing Scale, insight plays a very small role in this scale and is described in general terms that would not prove helpful to identifying insight in writing.

Snyder's Insight Measure cannot be considered for composition purposes because too little is known about his classification system and reliability and validity. Labov and Fanshel's linguistic analysis cannot be considered either because their system was never employed, thus no reliability can be calculated.

Several criteria can now be stated. In order to measure insight in student writing, an instrument should examine student writing (as opposed to modes of discourse students would not produce) and be valid and reliable. Table 3.4 displays the four tests and these criteria.

INSTRUMENT DEVELOPMENT

The decision to develop a scale to identify and measure insight in student texts was motivated by descriptions of insight by experts in psychology, philosophy, theology, and composition and by the patterns of personal discovery the researcher saw in student texts. As was discussed in Chapter 2, insight has prerequisites, qualities, and effects. There are degrees of insight; knowledge of the dimensions of insight enabled the researcher to recognize it in student texts.

Table 3.4. Methods of Analyzing Insight Versus Criteria for Composition Instruments.

Method	Addresses Writing	Validity	Reliability
Insight Measure (Snyder, 1945)		?	X
Experiencing Scale (Klein et al., 1969)		X	X
Therapeutic Impact Content Analysis System (Elliott et al., 1985)		X	X
Linguistic Analysis (Labov & Fanshel, 1977)		?	?

Over a period of 2 years, a scale was developed for insight. The process of instrument development is described in order to explain the scale and to guide other researchers interested in the process of measurement design.

Developing a scale for any construct begins by defining in specific terms, or operationalizing, that construct. After a researcher has identified the general domain of the construct, quantifiable indicators of the construct must be articulated. In this case, Chapter 2 presents the domain of the construct of insight. To articulate quantifiable indicators of insight in student texts, the researcher turned to students' expressive writing in which she postulated that the construct of insight might be explicitly articulated or easily inferred. Over a 2-year period she coded more than 200 expressive essays from students enrolled in basic and regular first-year composition courses at a large midwestern university. These courses were taught using a variety of teachers and pedagogies.

The researcher first intuitively sorted the essays into piles of "insightful" and "noninsightful" writing, using the entire student essay as the unit of analysis. The entire essay allowed her to view patterns of personal discovery that she might have overlooked in smaller units of analysis, such as words or sentences. In the "insightful" pile, she began noting any type of mental act—such as decisions, ideas, discoveries, imaginings, and so forth—as the grossest net of insight. What insightful papers had in common were expressions of new worlds, new understanding, action, and peace at resolving a dilemma.

The Insight Scale

After an intuitive sorting of students' papers and a literature search, the development of the Insight Scale was begun. Because the experts saw insight as resulting from a response to dissonance, the scale was developed (see Table 3.5) to show levels of dissonance resolution in written texts. What follows is an explanation of each level.

Level 4 is the complete resolution of dissonance, a full insight, whose features are described in Chapter 2. Writers admit complex dissonances, confront them with their whole selves, shift perspectives, and tell of seeing new worlds. Their essays usually provide the full context for their discovery; that is, writers present the dissonance and their own perspective before and after the insight. They relate a relatively simple solution to the complex

Table 3.5. Insight Scale.

O. No dissonance. (or) Vague essay, no resolution.

I. *Inadequate Resolution of Dissonance*
  a. Clear focus but the essay concerns another subject.

II. *Egocentric Resolution of Dissonance*
  a. Description in terms of the self only.
  b. Writer and subject locked into traditional roles.
  c. Dissonance seen as negative expectations; resolution is reversal of negative expectations.

III. *Incomplete Resolution of Dissonance*
  a. Missing information precludes a resolution.
  b. Parts of the dissonance recognized but not adequately explored in the paper.
  c. Resolution does not cover major parts of the dissonance.
  d. Several solutions offered.
  e. Admission of inability to resolve confusing aspects of the subject.

IV. *Complete Resolution of Dissonance*
  a. All aspects of the dissonance are encompassed in the resolution.
  b. Sense of rest and satisfaction at having resolved the problem.
  c. Rhythmic language at the end of the essay signaling finality.
  d. Subject viewed in an entirely new way.
  e. Whole context provided.
  f. Perspective-taking present. The writer can transcend his or her and others' roles.

---

problem, yet the solution encompasses many if not all facets of the dissonance. Writers express peace and satisfaction at having solved their problems. Often the ends of their essays contain rhythmic closes signaling the permanency of the discovery. Two examples of writing at this level follow.

Level 4 Sample Essay
The Class of '83 in '84

I suppose we were never warned because they knew we wouldn't listen. Or possibly they did tell us, but we refused to hear what they were saying. We, the Class of 1983, had become so overly involved with ourselves and the plans we had for our future that we never took the time to learn what the world was really like. We would be eternally young, carefree, and as united for the rest of our lives as we had been all during school.

My friends and I congregated in one classroom every morning to discuss how to dodge the principal, where we would go Friday night, and what we would do to the senile old nun who was our English teacher. These earth-moving decisions we made in the morning shaped the lives of all others in our little high school. After all, we were the mighty Seniors! God came to us for the answers! We were college-bound and ready to bring the world to its knees! We spent days in school and nights dreaming of how to rule our world the way we ruled our own little high school.

We knew of all things but our innocence, and we were too foolish to notice. Our parents had been protecting us for all of our lives. No one really knew what was outside the walls of childhood, and when the walls crumbled away, imagine the surprise we felt when our long rule had ended.

Within a few months after graduation, the great move began. Bags were packed, cars were loaded, and the past was left behind. We went to work, college, and into marriages. No matter what the move, the great rock that our parents had been no longer held us up. At long last we could make our own decisions on what to do about the day to day hassles of life. The only problem with making these decisions was that we were totally responsible for our own actions. No one was there to bail us out. It was not easy learning to wash our own clothes, keep our rooms clean, and do our work without being told eight times by a loving mother. Somehow, though, we managed, and along the way we changed.

Among the 39 people who graduated with me, 4 had to change—their soon to be born children would not allow them to remain as they were. College was shoved on the back burner indefinitely, and the frills of youth were left behind. No more all night parties—4 a.m. feedings take precedence.

Those who went to work and moved out found a new problem—loneliness. There were no parents butting in, no brothers and sisters starting fights, none of the things a family has to offer. To add to the isolation, those close friends weren't only a few minutes away—they had spread out across the Midwest. Few of the close relationships for which my class was known for could survive the distances which college caused, both in miles and points of view.

College had a way of changing one's perspective. We walked into a world full of books, strangers, and new ideas. Coming from a very small high school didn't prepare any of us for the 500 seated lecture halls or trying to find which building your next class is in. The new faces brought new perspectives and new challenges. Old ideas were hauled out to be tested and modified. None of us emerged from the first year of college unchanged.

And now, 1 year later, the changes are only too obvious. We are all so far from what we once thought we were. Some of the bonds between us have been broken beyond repair. I can't help feeling some sense of loss over the friends I left behind. Only those bound by ties of steel could survive the changes, and they have been rewarded by being even closer. Absence does seem to make the heart grow fonder, but only if people stay in touch. And for those who haven't made it out of our hometown, I can't help but feel some sorrow.

Our new lives have even affected our laughter. The hollow sound is gone from within. It has changed to the nervous laughter of strangers forced upon each other by the past. Whenever this barrier is transcended, the hollowness is replaced by the deeper tone of people who need to laugh with each other, if only to remember a common past. We laugh at the newness of our lives and the foolish attitudes we once had. But always there is some underlying hint of sorrow. We now need to laugh, it is the easiest way to share our memories.

Now the students among us trade horror stories of dorm food, all nighters, and the crazy guy down the hall. Those with families can only smile politely at the memories they will never have. Our paths have split after 12 years and only cross now at weddings and holidays. We have gone our separate ways, only to be joined at the end of our journeys.

Here is another Level 4 essay.

Level 4 Sample Essay

As time moves on and I become more aware of who I am and what I would like to accomplish, there are a few decisions that I have manufactured that I regret. Regret, or even better, repentance, are emotions that seem to design my college existence. As an eager freshman, I pledged an organization on this campus. I honestly wish that my mind and body would have been a little less present-oriented and a little more aware of what detrimental repercussions would occur through pledging. As much as I disagreed with the entire pledge process, including the intense labeling, I endured the rigorous process. Although my experiences fostered bitter feelings and a huge sense of hypocrisy, I saw it through till the end.

My pledging process was very similar to that of the Greek life on this campus. As a siblinghood, we had two pledge functions every week for 16 long weeks. The functions would begin with the pledge class being lined up like a bunch of pigs being prepared for slaughter. A sibling would approach the pledge class and attempt to alter our upbeat moods by telling us that we were not worth anything. The siblings would go on and recount all of the times, since the last function, that pledges had either been obdurate or been disrespectful to other siblings. Then like a mass of Holocaust victims, the pledges would be blindfolded and led into the house hearing messages in the air like, "It does not look so good for you, pledge," and "This pledge class is worthless." Yet I persevered through this verbal harassment and blindly believed that the organization that I was pledging was completely faultless and untainted.

After the pledge class would assemble in the house, each one of us would have to place our mouths at the end of the tap extended from the beer keg and drink until we were visibly full. Toward the end of the pledging there were a few of us who became wise and realized that you did not need to actually drink the beer. All you had to do was present a facade and pretend to drink with your cheeks bulging and looking like you were intensely inhaling beer. After about five trips to the keg for each pledge the rest of each function was different. The functions always involved a message that this siblinghood was entirely better than fraternities because it allowed women also. My siblinghood tried so creatively not to be like a fraternity that in essence, the real difference was not only could a pledge get verbally abused by men but women could haze a pledge too. Throughout the long term of being somehow subordinate to older and supposedly wiser hypocrites, I disagreed with many facets of this pledge process. The main problem that I am deliberating about is why I pledged an organization. I started pledging suspicious of the whole enterprise and any feelings of doubt were only enhanced by my experience.

In searching for answers to this qualm I have come to many stalemates concerning my emotions. In the long run, I am a sibling who is not active at all in the organization. Following my completion of our transparent pledge process I realized that in exercising my rights to flourish creatively and individually I had defaulted those values for a superficial welcome mat. I wanted to become appreciated and part of a growing group of individuals that were more profound than they were unenlightened. However, this organization has only endowed negative experiences in my life. I labeled myself when I graciously donned my pledge pin for all to see. This labeling is very detrimental to the subconscious of any 20-year-old who is going through major changes in maturing.

This important time in life is, in essence, finding out who you are and acting out your respective answers in an adult culture that maintains acceptance as the apex of its value structure. At the closure of my pledge process the identity that I was left with was of an individual who had forsaken the possibilities of questioning authority and seeking a lifestyle abundant in creative opportunities. I became a member of a group that delivered messages of hypocrisy and contradiction. The siblinghood was supposedly based on the theory of welcoming everyone with different opinions and different criticisms. I learned that my questions and opinions were disregarded by the same group of people that supported this theory.

Pledges are told that this organization is the most egalitarian entity on campus. Pledges are coaxed into believing that they have an actual voice within the pledge process. Nevertheless, pledges are told that they should only be seen in public with other pledges. Pledges are educated about the history of the organization in a very biased and unobjective light. All of these ideas that flow through the annals of this organization are contradicted in the pledge process by angry, chemically dependent hypocrites that prey on the naivete of their new pledges. Each pledge class is like a new life for the members that have already been through the process. By having a pledge class that does not question the manipulative motives of their teachers, the organization moves sadly forward with direction. I was a very inquisitive pledge and my curiosity served as a problem amongst the supposed open-minded siblings and myself. When I asked why a certain pledge was getting hazed for showing up to a meeting 2 minutes late, I was told to go fuck myself. When I asked why one of my friends was asked to leave the pledge class, I was told that it was not any of my business. How can an organization promote acceptance and diversity through the slight scope of being highly selective towards the people that want to become part of it?

My relationship with the majority of the people among the organization is on extremely false terms. My realization of the organization's transparency has influenced my present interaction with the siblings. Yesterday I was walking on the quad and ran into the current president. I could see her in the distance and I was preparing myself for a confrontation. There was no confrontation, just an extension of her middle finger in my direction. If a group genuinely desires diversity then people within its borders would be able to understand that what they may hold sacred to their hearts is not true of everyone that goes through a pledge process.

So I often ponder what motivated me to pledge an organization and then to become completely inactive after the whole process. I feel that as a sophomore I understand more about life than I did as a naive freshman. Sadly, all of the lessons that I was supposed to learn through my pledge process became lies on top of smaller lies. As a pledge you are nothing more than a lab rat that is looking for direction. I was a lab rat in a maze of different directions that were offered to me last year. I took part in degrading my own self-image to be one among many, rather than searching for my own identity through failure and success.

It is important in the present social structure which seems to fleetingly motivate our personal decisions, that being part of a group is a necessity that must be fulfilled in college. I thought that by pledging this organization, I would somehow achieve all of the emotions of comraderie and not be part of a negative social force. In attempting to fit among a group, I conformed to what they wanted me to be. The pledge process is designed to make the pledge believe that what he or she is trying to become part of is an answer and I have only found more and more questions through my experience.

Is there one solid answer to the question of why I pledged? In essence I pledged an organization different from a fraternity to escape conforming and yet, my pledge process preyed on each individual pledge to conform into something that hated everyone else that was not active or involved with their organization. On swing night, each individual pledge is brought into a room to hear that what they have just been through is probably the most important process that they have ever taken part in. When I had my personal meeting with the siblings, I was still verbally harassed even after the fact. My inactivity in this organization stems not only from disagreeing with the actual pledge process but also and more importantly, from a personal realization that being a wise and prosperous individual is a lot better than being a conformed alien.

Level 3 is an incomplete resolution of dissonance in a text, corresponding to the "false" or "intellectual" insight described by psychologists and to "inverse insight" as described by Lonergan (1957/1978). Writers acknowledge complex dissonances and either cannot resolve them because of circumstances beyond their control or produce temporary or intellectual solutions. Either case reveals the writer in a state of mental agitation rather than the peaceful attitude expressed by writers at the higher level. Also unlike Level 4 essays, Level 3 essays do not give the full context of insight because the insight event is not possible or not complete. A key to understanding the dilemma of these writers may lie in the degree to which they consider the problem with their whole selves. Level 3 papers are marked by their mental considerations as opposed to emotional ones or combinations thereof. An example of this level follows.

Level 3 Sample Essay

An annoying high pitch tone enters my brain and my arm automatically swings over and shuts off my alarm clock. I stare into the red glow and read the numbers, 5:45 a.m. The room is completely dark and I can hear my roommate slowly stir below as I throw back my covers and jump out of my loft. My feet land with an immense thud, my knees bend and my legs send a throbbing pain up to my brain. I lift up the shade to see that it is still dark out, the street lights are still on and a light rain is falling. My roommate turns on the light, I rub my eyes and quietly ask myself, why?

Why would any college student, or anyone in their sane mind, get up voluntarily at 5:45 in the morning? Simple, the love of a wonderful sport, crew. Actually it is not that simple, I am kind of confused about my feelings for crew, as most people get confused with things that they give so much to and care for. So as I slugglishly pull on my socks and slip on my sneakers, the question of why is becoming harder and harder to answer. Matt, my roommate, and I make our way across the street from our dorm to meet the rest of the team. As I greet the others with a yawn I am reminded that I am not alone. We quickly jump into our cars to escape the rain and make the 5 minute ride down to the boat house.

During the ride my mind starts to wander as the sound of

the rain on the windshield puts me in a dream state. I think back to my first morning practice. I was a junior in high school and I wanted to try something different, so I tried out for the crew team. I did not know many people but soon my fellow rowers became my friends. I loved getting up early and watching the sun rise over the harbor as we moved across the water which looked like a sheet of glass. A smile comes to my face as I remember how bad we were my first year rowing. I think we won one race but I did not care. I was having a wonderful time out in the fresh air feeling alive, feeling useful. Senior year was even better. My rowing improved and so did the team, we won most of our races and placed well in the New England Champions. We traveled to England to row at Henley and there I had the best 3 weeks of my life. I remember shedding a tear when our last race was over and I realized that I would never row with these friends again.

I am brought back to reality as the car hits a bump and my head smacks the window. Mike the driver, fellow rower and great friend, is complaining about the rain and the blisters on his hands. "Man, look at this one! This rain sucks, rowing in the cold rain just is not fun," says Mike in a still sluggish morning voice. The word "fun" goes echoing into my head as I slowly become hypnotized by the movement of the windshield wipers. I think back to freshman year when someone asked me if I was going to row at Hobart. I said sure, as long as I am having fun I will continue to row but when I stop having fun, I will stop rowing. Face it, no one wants to do something if it is not fun or worthwhile. Waking up at 5:45 in the morning and giving up your social life is not fun but rowing out on the water in perfect harmony with seven other rowers is. As we pull up to the boat house I silently ask myself, "am I still having fun."

I grabbed two oars from the rack and jog them down to the dock. As I put the oars down my eyes scan the canal and out of the corner of my eye I see a heron fly low across the water then up over the trees. I am reminded of how beautiful nature can be, even on a rainy day. Most of the students at school never see this canal or the gorgeous herons that inhabit it. I turn back and quickly jog to the boat house to escape the rain.

I sluggishly move my body through a series of stretches. It is unbelievable to think that all my muscles are sore, but they are. We, the lightweight eight, get together for our hands in. We stand in a circle and everyone puts their hand in the middle all on top of each other. We think of a common inspirational word, count 3 and scream that word hoping it will push our bodies through another day's practice. During the hands in my eyes wandered about the faces of my fellow rowers. I turned my head to view the heavyweight boat and I could only recall three rowers, who were the others?

My freshman year the team was tight, the Varsity 8 which I was a member of, had a unique bond. I made my best and most important friends, we were not that great of a team but we had lots of fun. We finished sixth in the state but our future looked bright with an amazing coach. Jim Joy, one-time national sculler and member of the Canadian Olympic Rowing coaching staff, arrived at Hobart the same year I did. He has transformed the team and I am lucky to have him as my coach.

Then in my sophomore year things did improve. I stroked the J.V. 8 and we had a wonderful season, finishing second in the state and ninth in the Dad Vails. But once again as the season ends I am saddened when some of my close friends graduate. Other things happened that year to get me depressed. I watched my roommate relieve his frustrations toward the school by transferring while I felt that crew was the only reason keeping me here.

[Mark couldn't finish this essay because he couldn't resolve the question of whether to keep rowing.]

Level 2 indicates an egocentric resolution of dissonance in a text. In other words, writers resolve dissonances by relating their immediate worlds and stereotypical judgments without changing or expanding their understanding. Their essays describe the subject in terms of the self alone and treat any persons, including the audience, as belonging to traditional roles. This level reflects the composition theories of Lunsford (1980), Kroll (1980), and Flower and Hayes (1980), who have written about egocentrism as a characteristic of basic writers. Two examples of Level 2 essays follow.

Level 2 Sample Essay

Indiana Beach

I enjoy going to amusement parks very much. I especially enjoy it when I go with my family or friends. I went to Indiana Beach in Monticello last year with some of my relatives. Indiana Beach is located in central Indiana in the country. The things that made me enjoy a day at Indiana Beach were my relatives and the unusualness of the park.

When I first was told that my family was going to spend a day at Indiana Beach I did not want to go. I did not know anything about the beach and I thought my relatives would bore me to death. I had seen commercials of the beach on TV and it looked boring. But when I got there I said "wow!" I had never seen a park like this one in my life. It had gigantic parks, golf courses, tennis courts, baseball fields, giant slides, store, rides, a lake, games, and nice restaurants. The park also had a disco night on Tuesday and Fridays. We had missed that because we went on Saturday. The rides were very exciting. It had go-carts, giant rides, and boat trips in the lake. I rode the go-carts about 20 times. The food was good. The views of the restaurants showed most of the rides and the lake. The lake was huge and it had many diving boards and slides.

It came as a surprise to me that my relatives made my day so fun. I only have a few cousins that are of the same age group, but they made it fun anyway. When we went on the go-carts we had a family race. I came in third or fourth place. After that we all went swimming in the lake. We played a game of water polo. I got some good exercise playing that game. After we got out of the lake we went to eat dinner and I stuffed myself.

After we had eaten, it was time to go home. I did not want to go and I did not know what made me enjoy myself so much. Was it the unusualness of the park or was it the good family fun that made me want to stay? Well whatever it was, someday I will go back, with my family.

Level 2 Sample Essay

As I sit now at my word processor my mind is filled with clutter. When I reflect on the difference between my life now, and my life when I was young the difference startles me. I wish sometimes that I could go back to those times in my childhood, when all was peaceful, when anything in the world seemed possible, and when anything I needed I could get from my loving family. I believe that the beach symbolizes as well as illuminates my youth. My childish free-spirited attitude, unconditional love for my family, and sense of inner peace are all reinforced while I am at the beach.

My life now is limited by what I can, and cannot do. I feel that there are restrictions on my actions, and on my words. As a child the beach represented a place full of fun, laughter, and freedom. I felt as though I could do anything while at the beach. I could play in the sand with my brother, swim when I wanted to, and lay in the hot summer sun. I look back on these times now, and realize how much I would love to go back to the carefree existence I had then. To feel the complete freedom, and lack of tension I felt then is a feeling I yearn for. It is very seldom for me presently to feel free and easy about my life. There always seems to be an element of tension, or some problem that is too overbearing for me to handle. During my summers on the beach as a child I never felt this way. Maybe that is because they didn't exist, but it is probably because I didn't know these types of worries, and problems could be so powerful in a person's life.

The beach is a place I can go to and feel peaceful, and feel that the world is peaceful. The sense of peace I get from the beach is a sense that does not exist in my life today. Peace used to be something I felt often, this is no longer true. I now always have something to do or have to go somewhere that restricts my ability to feel calm, or at peace with myself. The beach holds many memories for me of peaceful, happy, uncluttered times in my life. I hold these memories close to me, and think back to those happy memories when I am feeling confused, or uneasy with my life. The beach is now able to take me back to that peaceful time in my life, when my life was free of complication.

The main memory I have of the beach is the feeling of overwhelming support I had when I was there. My family and I used to spend every summer at the beach, and when I was there my family was all I needed. They were my world and as far as I was concerned they were all I would ever need to feel happy, and complete. As a child my family was the most special element of my life. When we were all at the beach together I was the happiest child in the world. I wish now that I could go back to that time when my family was all I needed. I wish I could still rely on them for everything.

As I get older I feel as though I have so many responsibilities. I wish that my family could sometimes still shelter me in the same way they did when I was a child. I know, however, that I must face up to my responsibilities as an adult, and realize that I can no longer rely on my family to give me everything that I need. I do think of these summers on the beach with my family when I need to be back in that mind frame of security.

The beach provides me with many images that relate to my youth. Inner peace, my family, and a sense of freedom are the things I value most in this world. The beach is one place on this earth where I felt all of these important elements of my life in one place. I think of the beach, and go there as often as I can because it will always remain a place of joy, and peace to me.

Level 1 is an inadequate resolution of dissonance in a text. A text is scored at this level when the writer articulates a focus or thesis that expresses some dissonance that is not taken up in the essay. An example of such a thesis would be "At the beach I lose all sense of mortality." The essay discusses the beach at night, sounds on the beach, and privacy on the beach, but it never explores the relationship between the beach and the writer's experience there. The reader is left to conclude that the writer may have a dissonance worth exploring, but that the essay cannot be considered an adequate resolution of that dissonance. The following is an example of a Level 1 essay.

Level 1 Sample Essay

The Beach

I think the happiness that I get from being at the beach is so great that I just lose all sense of mortality. All my feelings are just dropped along with all my problems and worries that persist me. Many times I would be in very depressing moods or the atmosphere of the beach just seems to overcome my problems. Seeing the water wash ashore is very beautiful to watch because it makes you think. You think about your happy times and not about the times [*sic*].

Sounds from the beach help the setting of the beach to become even more pleasant. The sounds are very quiet no shouting and screaming just sounds of the waves. While during the day you can bearly hear because of radios and people screaming.

The setting of the beach is very pleasant in contrast to day time. Mainly because at night the moonlight is out and only Chicago and moon are visible to your eye. The nighttime sets the mood to be very romantic and peaceful.

The privacy you get from the beach is something you get and that's something you don't get at home. All the privacy you want is at the beach at the right time night time as preferred by me. You may want to talk to a girl or something is just think by yourself and the beach gives you this preferably at night.

The beach can be a very beautiful place to be in relation to these parts. The water to watch the water wash ashore is beautiful to watch and see. The sound of the beach is very pleasant also because you are quiet there is no shouting and screaming going on at night preferably. The setting helps by being on the moonlight and Chicago being in your vision. Finally the privacy you get from the beach is something that many people look for. I think the beach is the ideal place to be.

Level 0 is the absence of dissonance in a text. Writers treat topics as steady and unchanging. The way they understand subjects at the beginning of their essays remains the same at the end. They express none of the perceptions of writers at higher levels in the scale. A sample of this level follows.

Level 0 Sample Essay

The Computing Center Tour

The tour which I took in the math science building can be broken into several parts.

The first part of the computer center tour was getting to the basement. We had to go down two flights of stairs to get to the basement level. The first room we entered was the computer terminal room. There was about 30 terminals in all and almost all of them were in use. There were many people working quickly to get something done.

The tour then went into the printing room which is next to the terminal room. In the room were big racks that were stuffed with papers and folders. There were so much paper in the folders I couldn't see how it would all fit. In another room behind the racks were people who would get papers that printed on the printer and put them in the folders that whoever printed it out could pick it up. On the other side of the room is a punch card machine. It look old fashioned compared to all the other machinery but some people still use it for certain machines.

The tour went down the hall from the printing room into the information room. There were big file cabinets in the room. Inside the file cabinets were many papers on just about anything you would want to know about the computer system at Purdue. The papers are free and anyone who needs information is welcome to take what papers they want.

The tour went to a different floor and into a hallway. Down the hallway were many big windows. Through the windows there was a large room filled with many computers and storage devices. No one was allowed into the room because of certain security reasons, but we could still observe them through the window. Along the back of the wall was tape drives and huge racks of tapes. By requesting one of the tapes at a terminal someone will get the tape off the rack and put it on the tape drive so that you can use it.

Past the window the tour went into a similar room filled with computers. The computers were not what I had expected. Instead of a bunch of flashy lights and video screens there were a bunch of big rectangular shaped boxes that looked like refrigerators or washing machines. The computer which sounded like refrigerators have built in air conditioning to keep them cool. The computer needs a certain temperature and humidity to make them operate properly.

Around the room are disk drives that can send and receive data very fast. The disk drives use hard disks with six layers of records staked on top of each other to form one large disk that can hold millions of bits of data.

The floor of the room is strange. The floor is raised so that wires can run underneath it. That way wires wouldn't be all over the floor. When you walk on the floor it squeaks and you can feel it move a little bit.

In one section of the room is a large computer called the CYBER 205. This computer can hold millions and millions of data characters by itself without any storage devices. The CYBER 205 is so fast that it can perform a single instruction in only nine nano-seconds which is nine millionths of a second.

New computers are being developed all the time. When they have the next tour I'll be sure to be in it.

Training Raters

Although the scale provides guidelines for discriminating among student essays, raters must be trained to recognize levels with accuracy. The use of as many raters as possible increases the reliability according to the Spearman-Brown Prophecy Formula. The researcher began with five raters who are composition specialists and experienced teachers.

An important part of the training was the raters' ability to recognize their own preconceptions toward insight. The group discussed various insights of each member while the researcher put qualities of their insights on a blackboard. Rather than lecture about insight, the researcher wanted raters to acknowledge and expand their current understanding of it according to her specific definitions. This session also allowed the researcher to identify raters who did not have a clear understanding of insight as defined by the scale.

Raters were directed to read the last paragraph of a student essay first to decrease reading time and to direct the reader to the insight. Instead of reading from the beginning of the essay, raters looked in the last paragraph for verbal cues about the level of insight achieved. Some verbal cues that correspond to levels of insight are presented in Table 3.6. With a guess as to the level of insight, the raters were told to skim the rest of the essay for descriptors associated with that level.

One of the most important features of an instrument is its reliability; that is, the extent of agreement reached by raters using the instrument to differentiate student texts. An acceptable level of reliability for an instrument in development stages is .60 and above. This feature guarantees that the instrument's levels are clearly enough explained and differentiated by the researcher so that others can reach agreement assigning a level to each essay.

Table 3.6. Verbal Cues of Insight

Level 4	"I finally realized that . . . " "I now understand that . . . " "All of a sudden it hit me . . . "
Level 3	"Maybe . . . " "I guess . . . " "I guess I'll never know why . . . " "I wonder why . . . "
Level 2	"X wasn't like I thought it would be." "Now everything will be like it was." "X person is a (traditional role) to me." Last paragraph contains discovery related to self and/or traditional roles if appropriate to paper topic.
Level 1	Last paragraph contains no mental conclusion. Usually a description. The reader's reaction should be "so what?" Rater should review thesis for dissonance. If thesis contains dissonance, the paper is scored as Level 1.
Level 0	Last paragraph is the same as Level 1. If thesis contains no dissonance, the paper is scored as Level 0.

Establishing Reliability

The essays used to establish reliability were gathered from four classes of first-year composition taught at a large midwestern university ($n = 100$). Four raters, experts in composition theory and teaching, received 4 hours of training using the insight scale. The researcher led the training and rating sessions. Raters compared scores after every 5 papers, but retained the original ratings. By the end of 20 papers, the interrater reliability reached a sufficiently high level (Cronbach's $\alpha = .91$).

The next chapter presents a second measurement instrument for insight in writing.

4

Insight Test

This chapter is not directed at statisticians and educational psychologists, but instead at the lay reader. Readers of the former ilk can consult an earlier work (Murray, 1987), wherein all the testing details are manifest. This chapter is based on the classic text *Psychometric Theory* by Nunnally (1978) and is augmented by the work of Geisinger (1992) and Messick (1988); anyone wishing to expand their reading on this topic might begin with Asher (1976), Kerlinger (1986), and Nunnally. In order that readers may have some understanding of the process of test construction and that they may appreciate how this one was composed, the qualities of a good test and the tale of this one are discussed. At this still early stage in the development of the field of rhetoric and composition, readers may wish to use this chapter to envision testing possibilities for interests of their own.

DETESTING TESTING

Many readers come to this subject a bit askance. In the not too distant past, former President George Bush considered nationwide testing, evoking caustic reactions from many educators. The egregious errors are well known: These tests are sexist and racist; they "objectify" knowledge that we wish were known in a deeper and more expansive way; they set limits on lives; and they generate too fat profits for "nonprofit" testing agencies.

Nonetheless, something must be working to enable the testing empire in this country to conquer the way it does. That something is the elegance and simplicity of psychometrics, which is analogous to the world of ballet. Like ballet, it is a solidly known field with procedures that are clear and readily employed. Also like ballet, it stymies those who wish for greater range of expression while it enthralls those who can appreciate the great difficulty of mastering technique and making it appear graceful and elegant.

Where skeptical readers can meet psychometricians is at the point of content. Where testing goes awry is in false or impoverished content; more than any other feature, a test's content determines its worth. Similarly, all the technique in the world will never make a dancer. A spirited dancer controls and employs technique; it is his or her inner qualities (largesse, finesse, grace of interpretation) that make a dancer, not knowledge of pliés, développées, chassées. The same maxim can be yielded for testing: A thorough, complete understanding of the content must underlie a test, for all the technical mastery of statistics will never make it a sound one.

Now for the odd paradox: Unfortunately, it is not the other way around. Solid content does not a test make. Reconsider the dance analogy. Witness an average 4-year-old dancing with all the gusto she possesses, or imagine the performance of an average student in a college modern dance class. Neither has mastered technique, and without it, the dance is usually frenzied and of poor quality. Similarly, no matter how venerable the content, if the statistics or machinery of the test is not in order (mastered, if you will), the test too will be poor in quality and basically will not function.

May it then be asked whether excellent content and smooth running statistics would make racism, sexism, and so forth vanish from exams? Only if excellent content is directed fairly at the test takers. Frequently, test writers do not employ the methods that are discussed shortly. Instead, something like the following happens: Test composers focus on the mathematical elegance and efficiency of a multiple choice question (the statistics are lovely); thousands of students take these questions and the results are studied—items dropped or recomposed, and the trial runs go on; eventually a mathematically beautiful but meaningless test surfaces. No theory concerning the subject to be tested is ever consulted. Moreover, the lack of employing test writers from various racial, ethnic, class, and social groups and the lack of concerning these test writers with students' test-taking experiences cause most of the problems we see today. A more dramatic illustration is in order.

This dilemma is taken from the field of psychoanalysis, courtesy of eminent statistician Gene Glass. A multitrait/multimethod 10,000 word report (i.e., a staggering amount of time and energy) was expended on scores from a test of "self-concept." The findings? Self-concept comes from experiences with the environment and from interactions with "significant others." If such a statement seems at once obvious and nebulous, Glass agrees. Pointing out the paucity of research on the concept of self (the one notable study having been written in the last century), Glass identified the idiocy of refluxing highly complex statistical procedures on very little content. Glass's (1986) comments are well worth considering:

> Clearly, this is a picture of psychometrics running amuck! Big methodological guns loaded with folk wisdom and truisms. This factor analytic mincing could go on forever; we could, of course, equally well discover "automobile self-concept," "favorite football team self-concept," or even "preferred Baskin-Robbins flavor self-concept."
>
> The problem with this empirical hustle and bustle is that it is thoroughly innocent of any serious theory about the psychological sense of self; how it develops, what it is, how it can become sick, how to make it well. How adequately do the Rogerian theory and the other commonsense accounts of "self-concept" stand up to the "risky" tests of explanatory scope which alone will separate idle psychologizing from respectable theory, such risky tests as accounting for the ephemeral sense of identity of a thoroughly decompensated schizophrenic, the sense of gender identity so confused as to cause a man willfully to mutilate his body surgically and chemically, the dangerous line between positively cathected self-representations and neurotic narcissism, the splintered selves of a multiple personality, or the more ordinary feelings of depression and emptiness in a child whose every act prompts nothing but praise and reward from the "significant others" of [his or her] environment? Unless our theories reach this far, they are in jeopardy of being not so much false as uselessly redundant with ordinary common sense. (p. 20)

To repeat, it is content, along with statistics, and along with concern for the test taker that make the test. It is now important to consider, with this caveat, what "good" means in regard to a test.

WHAT IS A GOOD TEST?

A good test is reliable and valid not only in an abstract or independent sense, but also in its responsibility toward the persons the test is designed to address. If a test is given to faculty regarding leadership, and the majority have great leadership skills, but the test is in Swahili, the test may be reliable and valid, but responsible only to those faculty speaking Swahili. A test designer must look at the interrelationship of these elements when composing a test.

The purpose of a test is to discriminate, thus a reliable test is expected to discriminate among test takers in different circumstances. Just as a reliable vehicle performs in icy as well as in favorable weather, a reliable test will function appropriately time after time. If the test is given next Friday afternoon or 3 years from now, the results should be similar. As in the car analogy, reliability is an internal matter: The car is reliable because its engine, battery, and oil work together well to start the car. Similarly, the items working together to contribute to the total test score is what makes a test reliable. If the battery is dead, the car will not start. If a number of items do not contribute to the total test score, the test will not be reliable.

An example of how a test can be unreliable is when various items detract from the total test score. If several items are so poorly worded that no reader can consistently tell what they mean, then the results of the scores from that item will be such a confusing array that the item itself will detract from the total test score. When these items do not contribute to the total test score but exhibit a dispersed set of scores of their own, they cause the test to be unreliable.

Thankfully, psychometricians have done such exemplary work on reliability that very reliable tests can be made. The mathematics, which are eminently controllable, account for this accuracy. Reliability can be measured quite clearly, and in fact, the bulk of the psychometrician's time is spent on reliability matters. The reasoning behind this concentration of time is that no test is worth anything if it is not reliable first, no matter how rich in content. As Charlie Brown so aptly put it, "how could we lose when we were so sincere?"

Test validity refers to the match between the test items and what the test purports to measure compounded with how likely test takers are to understand and respond appropriately to those items (Geisinger, 1992). Thus, validity and reliability issues blend when those who give tests try to ascertain whether a test is "good." Good must encompass the test takers, the test itself, and the individual items on the test. If, for instance, the test itself was faithful to the matter it measured, but students found the items too difficult to understand, the testing situation is not good. Test designers and those who employ tests must also consider the social consequences of the testing situation and not merely whether the reliability figures and the validity checks point to a good test. The glamour, if you will, of the elegant mathematical procedures seduces many into playing with test machinery before they spend great amounts of time establishing the validity of the content.

Validity needs to be a matter of consideration before, during, and after test construction. Attending to a test's validity before considering reliability issues is the most creative and challenging aspect of test composition, especially when the construct is ill defined.

As in the case that Glass cited, it would be foolish to try to establish validity after that reliable but meaningless test on self-concept was devised. The way to establish validity throughout the test construction process is to begin with valid information. Nunnally (1978), author of the classic text *Psychometric Theory*, advised creating an outline of the content before any work on the actual test begins. This outlining is a very creative venture, for the content is usually determined by a number of experts coming at the test from either usage or expertise in the subject area. A ninth-grade algebra test, for instance, might draw its content from the following sources: a compilation of problems found in textbooks, teachers' suggestions, suggestions from business and technical people in the community whose businesses use algebra, mathematics professors, educational consultants, and so forth. The wide array of sources yields the perspectives needed for creating valid content.

Psychometricians speak of valid content as a domain. The terms *universe* or *population* from statistics equal the term *domain*; most experimentation is based on the logic that only a sample of a larger population is studied for various reasons (like the sheer impossibility of studying the population, or the lack of need to do so). Test constructors use the same logic when they speak of a domain: The domain is the exhaustive set of features that describes the subject of the test. For an algebra exam, the domain would be all algebra problems that ninth graders should know how to solve (of course some more difficult items are added just to differentiate among very high scoring students).

When the subject of the test is far less quantifiable than algebra problems, circumscribing the domain becomes a great challenge. When researchers want to test a more diffuse subject, like depression for instance, or success, they have even more content outlining to do. When a subject to be studied is not exceedingly quantifiable, but rather is a label for a set of symptoms or phenomena, psychometricians refer to it as a *construct.* No one knows what depression is; we cannot see it or weigh it, but psychologists have so adequately studied its accidents that we now have valid and reliable tests for it. No one knows what the flu is (or any number of diseases); we cannot see or weigh that either, but medical researchers and pharmacologists have described the set of symptoms so well that tests and medicines are based on their work. When a researcher wants to test a construct, the construct itself must be well understood. Thus, it becomes readily understandable why the example Glass cited failed: Few researchers had mapped out the complex construct of self and therefore the testing researchers could not form an adequate domain.

A cry usually goes up when some important but understudied constructs become the subjects of tests. Thurstone (1959), in his classic text *The Measurement of Values*, noted that more than 30 years ago psychological constructs were thought to be incapable of being measured:

> Psychological theory can be rigorous. There is an erroneous impression among psychologists, as well as among our academic neighbors, that psychological ideas are necessarily loose, verbal, subjective, and unfit for the quantitative analytical treatment of science. This impression is not justified. It is not necessary for us to abandon psychological concepts if we introduce analytical rigor in dealing with these concepts. (p. ii)

The most challenging issue regarding psychological tests today is not their analytical rigor so much as their inherent bias. That is, Thurstone was right—psychological constructs can be tested for in reliable and valid ways. The sophistication of the testing and labeling process of psychologists attests to this; nevertheless, whole tests and diagnoses can be perfectly valid and reliable but fail to address the test taker or the social consequences of the test itself. Tavris (1992), in her book *The Mismeasure of Woman*, cited the codependency movement as inherently biased against women because it is based on the male norm of autonomy. Similarly, tests for women's psychological health may do no more than reveal how nonmale women are and therefore deem them "unhealthy." Thus, the issue facing test constructors currently is to design and validate their tests contextually: Persons ultimately take these tests and no amount of technical sophistication can deny the use to which the test is put. Geisinger (1992) traced the development of test validation citing the movement from atheoretical and acontextual conceptions of validity to the more context-bound concerns of late. Although still a debated and complex subject, test validation promises to secure more fair tests in the future.

Tests in rhetoric and composition are biased not so much from the gender viewpoint as from the traditional conception of writing as style. The average person thinks of writing as a matter of stylistic and grammatical correctness or as a mysterious, inspired "gift." Correspondingly, most tests of English, even composition tests, are tests of grammar because of two well-known facts: Grammar is easily scored and English instructors look for it when scoring essays (Diederich, 1974). The magical gift of writing is thought to be untestable and certainly impossible to score.

Testing agencies and school administrators often brag that composition tests are not necessary: They cite the high correlations between composition and grammar tests and reason that they can simply employ tests of grammar. Grammar tests seem more efficient and economical, yet the issue is one of constructs. The constructs that rest within a written essay are many and they have yet to be mapped out in terms of their domains. So rather than grapple with a measurement task that is simply overwhelming, many readers in English opt for grammatical prowess as an indicator of good writing skill.

Does this mean that various interesting but elusive constructs (such as writing quality or insight or audience adaptation) cannot be quantified and tested? No, but it does mean that much library research into the desired constructs must precede any efforts at test construction. Given the limited studies in our field of rhetoric and composition, such efforts demand interdisciplinary research.

The check at the end of the test-composing process that one's efforts at defining the construct are sound was once simply referred to as *construct validity*. Construct validity entailed comparing test scores of the construct in question to similar and dissimilar constructs; one could be somewhat assured of construct validity if the scores of the construct in question were not duplicated by a test of a similar construct, or if scores from a test of a construct one considered opposing the construct in question did in fact radically differ from the test scores of the construct in question. Nevertheless, as much discussed in the literature, such a process of comparisons can be endless, and thus construct validity can never truly be established once and for all. Messick (1988) enhanced the process of test validation at the end of the testing process by stipulating that researchers must account not only for construct validity in the traditional sense, but also for the meaning of the scores to society and for their practical social consequences. He clarified the overall process in Figure 4.1:

	Test Interpretation	Test Use
Evidential Basis	Construct Validity	Construct validity + Relevance/Utility
Consequential Basis	Value Implications	Social Consequences

Figure 4.1. Messick's (1980) Facets of Test Validity

Published in R. Wainer & H.I. Braun (Eds.), *Test validity*. Hillsdale, NJ: Erlbaum. Reprinted with permission of the publisher.

According to Messick, the evidential basis for test validation is comprised of traditional construct validity alongside the proof of relevance/utility. *Relevance/utility* refers to the correspondence between the form of the test and the content (e.g., a multiple-choice test of grammar given to discriminate among students' writing ability suffers a lack of relevance/utility).

It is the consequential basis of test interpretation and test use that are more recently proposed by testing researchers such as Messick. To establish value implications means to be able to articulate clearly what the score means for society, what it means in terms of the test interpretation theory, and what it means in terms of the ideologies underlying the test interpretation theory (Messick, 1988, p. 20). In short, one must locate the meaning of the test score at multiple levels—both within the explanatory power of the test theory and outside the theory in the ideologies driving the test. An extended study of the value implications of the construct of intelligence is found in Gould (1981) *The Mismeasure of Man*. From their onset, Gould explains, intelligence tests have been racist and sexist. That such testing could be so pervasive and long lasting makes Gould's work especially important to society as a whole.

The consequential basis of test use is a practical accounting for the "potential and actual social consequences of the applied setting" (Messick, 1988, p. 20). These consequences would include pedagogical adaptations to the test, labels students might receive from the scores, the impact on minorities, and so forth (Geisinger, 1992, p. 210).

Test validation takes years to establish and thus, given the entire spectrum of test-making procedures (establishing content validity, reliability, and the various facets of test validity), such research is long and time consuming. Despite the length of time developing a good test takes, the benefits still outweigh the time spent. The gains to be had from testing are in the clarity with which we understand difficult constructs, increased research into the clarified constructs, speed in diagnosis, and far less bias in diagnosis (many studies in educational psychology confirm these findings).

This section has been a broad overview of how good tests are constructed and what characterizes them as good. Now for the tale of this particular test with an eye toward enabling researchers in rhetoric and composition to develop other kinds of tests.

THIS TEST'S PURPOSE

When considered from the previous paradigm (that writing is a matter of style and grammar), this test has no purpose whatsoever and may even be deemed unsubstantial. In that paradigm, it makes no sense to speak of the experience of learning that can come from writing nor does it make sense to speak of insight. The experience of insight in writing is relegated in that paradigm to persons of genius or those with natural gifts. When the paradigm is shifted, and writing is considered a creative process that involves much more of the human person, then a test for insight seems more appropriate, but perhaps still nebulous.

Two comparisons may help. A ninth-grade algebra test serves to discriminate among the abilities of students for a very good reason: Algebra is the foundation of all future mathematics and is in itself a logical means of manipulating symbols and solving problems. Not to discriminate among students regarding their mastery of algebra would be to send students into courses without knowing whether they fully understand the necessary backdrop of mathematics. Insight in college writing is also a kind of foundation that currently is missing in higher education.

Even so, this test for insight does not perform the gate-keeping function that the algebra test does. The mindset toward testing itself needs a new model. The second comparison is that of the "well child" examinations that are currently given to prevent the development of serious illness. Instead of being summative and punative, this free examination helps alert parents to any future problems and ensures sound development. Likewise, this test for insight in writing points toward increasing the quality of the intellectual life of students. Rather than hope that a few achieve insights, educators in college settings can begin—with this tool—to analyze a myriad of situations that either foster or hinder the experience of insight in writing.

The meaning of the score on this test—if considered from the previous paradigm—may also seem nonsensical. In most cases, grammar is either right or wrong; style is frequently appropriate or not so. The experience of insight, however, fits on a continuum: It is meaningful to speak of degrees of the resolution of dissonance rather than a simple resolution or the absence thereof. The score also reflects what is known as a *self-report:* Students identify their experience rather than have their insight judged by an outside person. The score gives educators information about whether students are considering rich and meaningful dissonances and working to resolve them. In many cases in college education, this kind of advanced consideration is exactly what the professor wishes. That is why this test is valuable and that is what its purpose is.

CIRCUMSCRIBING THE DOMAIN OF INSIGHT

As Nunnally stated, the first step of test construction is to outline the content and in so doing to consult the widest array of experts possible. In 1983, I began consulting literature in psychology only to be disappointed. Little work had been done on insight, although there were a few very important studies. Roback (1974) provided an overview of the insight literature noting that the term was "nebulous" at best but employed by psychologists of all schools. Nevertheless, the description of insight from those few sources matched my independent coding of insight in student essays. Even that small but important amount of work done in psychology was helpful, and so the studies of insight continued.

Because a clear description of insight could not be developed from the literature in psychology, I took an interdisciplinary approach including the fields of rhetoric and composition, theology, philosophy, and education. The results of this undertaking can be found in Chapter 2. Because the topic of insight is so understudied, only those descriptions of insight that were agreed on by experts in two or more fields were included in this study. That is, I reasoned that the information from scholars working independently who discovered the same things was a good verification of the qualities of insight. These 16 features form the domain of insight.

Some of the challenges and dangers encountered are important to recount here. The most notable is certainly the challenge of working with complex materials in unfamiliar disciplines. The only antidote to distortion is to seek assistance (which I did) through taking classes in other areas whenever possible, through consulting with professors, and through reading interpretations of important works. Again, the trade-off for interdisciplinary work of this nature is time.

Another challenge and danger is the necessity of researching the goals of each of the disciplines consulted. It is not enough to ascertain the findings of other disciplines: One must uncover the values spurring the research. Such study often yields great clarity to the construct being considered. Chapter 1 explores the goals of other disciplines regarding insight.

ESTABLISHING RELIABILITY

Once content representativeness is assured through the description of the domain, reliability procedures can begin. These procedures build a test that is likely to yield the same results in different circumstances. Once they are complete, the test items are subject to scrutiny regarding their ability to contribute to the test score as a whole.

Designing Items

Most readers have been exposed to a variety of test formats: yes-no, true-false, fill in the blank, multiple choice, range responses, and so forth. Most have probably been frustrated too at some point with the way a question was worded, such that the response one would like to give was not one of the possible choices. Deciding on the format and the wording of test items is the first step in establishing reliability. They are very closely related.

The greatest challenge, claimed Nunnally, is to avoid vagueness and ambiguity. In general, the ways to do so are to have a number of people compose items and to pilot test them. Although I began testing wording and format together, for the sake of clarity they are discussed separately.

Wording.

Nunnally (1978) said that well-worded items are neither ambiguous nor trivial; instead they guide the respondent to the desired response (p. 259). The challenge in the task of wording items is to remain faithful to the theoretical descriptor (in this case one of the 16 features) in language that the user can understand. Considering that the term *insight* has such a variety of popular meanings, this was quite a challenge.

To discover what types of wording to use, I drew up an open-ended questionnaire that covered only the most agreed on features of insight. That is, each item on the questionnaire was followed by a "comments" section that asked respondents to clarify their response or react to the item; this ability to respond further is what is meant by "open-ended." By developing this initial questionnaire, I hoped I could then select an appropriate format. Once an appropriate format is selected (e.g., true-false), responses can be assigned numbers (e.g., zero for true and 1 for false) and analysis for reliability begins.

This first attempt at designing a test was playful and unstructured. I not only proceeded as directed by Nunnally, but also followed hunches, doubted my statistical and mathematical training, and pursued my own ideas about insight. Alongside items that corresponded to theories of insight from noted scholars, I added items of my own that corresponded to no theory or pushed at psychometric ways of composing items. Such play was very reassuring, however, because the items that surfaced as soundly representing insight did in fact conform to what Nunnally and other statistical sources said they would; whereas my own hypotheses and my tests of test construction theory were resoundingly smashed.

To my good fortune, I was teaching a night class of adult continuing education students who were the perfect test case. This kind of group is excellent for preliminary testing. These adults, unlike many 18- to 22-year-olds, were anything but afraid of their young teaching assistant and volunteered their comments on wording quite readily and in a more articulate way than their 18-year-old counterparts.

Important findings regarding wording were twofold: Items needed to be worded in simple terms and they could not contain the term *insight*. Experimenting with the wording of this open-ended questionnaire made apparent how useless the term *insight* is for testing purposes; its popular meanings are too varied for reliable responses. What follows is a brief example of the my trespassing every law of test construction only to learn lessons the hard way. In the sample item presented here, I am fascinated by the places where insights occur and thought my students would more readily admit their insights if questioned about the place. I was sure older students would discuss them with others as well. No theory undergirds either hypothesis. I was terribly wrong but learned a few things. Here is the item:

> I would have loved to discuss this insight with someone
> (a) but I was in the shower, or Sears, or picking up my
> kids when it happened.
> (b) so I ran out and grabbed someone to tell.
> (c) no, I really didn't want to share it.
> (d) no insight to share!
> (e) but there I was at my desk writing and nobody was
> around.
> Comments:

The "comments" line asks students to respond in prose to the item; the following are three responses:

1. "I guess when I wrote this essay I wrote it and was amazed at what I had written. I am beginning to realize now what all I really think instead of letting them pass over and forget them."

2. "My husband reads *almost* all my papers and critiques them. When you see checks in the margins those are his marks. I sometimes forget to erase them."

3. "I don't think anyone but me would appreciate the insight because only I have experienced and reacted to the lake."
   (Note: This student, unlike the others, circled the "no insight to share" alternative.)

These three responses to the same item illustrate what "wildly unreliable" means. The first one gets at the insight experience, but the second is totally out of place, and the third indicates a confusion between a personal insight and the need to share it or even conceive of it as one if it is to be shared. Coupled with the findings regarding the format that is discussed next, I decided that the Likert-type response would afford the simplicity and range of responses that these students indicated that they needed.

Item Format. Two types of formats were tried in the open-ended questionnaire—multiple-choice and true-false—because I was following Nunnally's chapter devoted to construction of multiple-choice exams. Nunnally (1978) stated that multiple-choice tests can measure almost anything given adequate content coverage and clear wording (p. 259). But multiple-choice items were ruled out here because students attached too many and varied comments to the items in the open-ended questionnaire, indicating that a few alternatives could not assess adequately the phenomenon of insight. In addition to writing comments, some subjects also circled more than one response. An example of this difficulty can be seen in the responses to the following item that is concerned with the feature of dissonance:

Is this really a touchy subject for you?
(a) Yes, and it's still touchy.
(b) Yes, but I really wanted to figure it out.
(c) No, it's not a touchy subject.
(d) No, it's an engaging, challenging subject.
(e) Not really touchy, but something I've always wondered about.
Comments:

Here are five comments from students:

1. "This is one of those subjects that people can't really understand how you feel or what you're going through until they've walked in your shoes."
2. "This is a subject that has created a lot of emotional conflicts for me—how can you love and hate someone at the same time?"
3. "I just have to figure it out for myself. It was too painful, I should not have tried to write about it."
4. "I am not certain if any of the above are applicable. It was neat to put it in writing. I think that's where it is."
5. "Annoying sometimes, but not touchy."

Respondents added comments revealing degrees of dissonance that the multiple-choice item did not gauge well enough. The degrees of dissonance reported by students led me to adopt Likert-type items in which subjects mark the degree of a dimension rather than opt for a set alternative.

The true-false item also drew a range of responses. One true-false item was included to force respondents to state clearly whether they had had an insight or not:

> True or False: I've reached a totally new understanding of this topic—something I've never seen before. Comments:

Respondents had difficulty with this question; a number of them expressed the need for a level in between reaching a totally new understanding (true) and not having one at all (false). As two respondents commented:

1. "Not necessarily a new understanding but a better understanding. . . . Probably because paper caused more awareness."
2. "I wouldn't say a totally new understanding, but feel one has to express themselves and putting your feelings down on paper certainly can help."

This true-false item, therefore, demonstrated the need for a graded item like a Likert-type scale that would allow the respondent to report the degree of presence of the dimension under study.

A Likert-type item is a brief statement to which the respondent agrees or disagrees. The degrees of agreement and disagreement vary, but usually tests employing Likert-type items provide respondents with five to seven degrees such as *strongly agree, agree, neutral, disagree*, and *strongly disagree.*

MORE VALIDITY MATTERS

Deciding to go on with the testing procedure was really neither a matter of wording nor format. Although these two things helped me focus on reliable items, it was more the tallying of the exams that verified the goal of being able to identify the construct of insight in a test form. The tallying of exams and the psychological descriptions of insight were parallel, establishing an early degree of content validity; the decision to use a Likert-type format met the relevance/utility need that Messick urged.

In order to be certain that the exams that would be analyzed for further test development did indeed relate the insight experience, I classified as "insightful" only those exams in which students answered positively to three items. All the items on the open-ended questionnaire dealt with insight, and the exam itself was short (11 items). Exams with such choices were clearly about the insight experience. Exams with two or less positive answers I marked "partial insight"; no positive answers were marked "no insight"; and any answers that indicated that the insight was had previous to the writing experience I set apart from my studies (e.g., if the student wrote about an insight he or she had 5 years ago).

The comments on those tests in the "insight" pile matched the literature on insight I had consulted. The following are a few of the maximlike sentences that surfaced:

1. "Independence is something you find within yourself and success is something you achieve."
2. "It made me think about my deep inner feelings and how I really feel about the world, people, and I learned something about myself."
3. "I find I approach some things in an almost artistic way. A philosophical insight is there: a love of beauty and perhaps an acceptance of reality. Quite frankly, I was surprised I like my own 'stuff' Ho!"

Writing was having an effect on the adult night class in terms of the insight experience. Notice how the whole self is involved in all three responses (it is present in ones not listed,too). Notice also that the insight experience is a new understanding that is radically different from the previous way of seeing things, or, is a grasping of what was already known. A set of students were making important personal discoveries through writing, and the research was helping to identify them. It also helped identify students who did not achieve insight for a variety of reasons. This ability to discriminate among students regarding how writing did or did not lead to insight is what a test should do.

CONSTRUCTING THE LIKERT-TYPE PILOT TEST

The function of a pilot test is to ascertain whether the length of the test, the wordings, and the item types will function in accord with the measuring of the construct desired. In order to keep the test duration short, I began with 30 items. The items were worded by fellow graduate students in rhetoric and composition and by me. The Likert-type item was selected because it allowed for a range of responses; students indicated they needed such a range in the prior study.

Considering the large set of dimensions of insight, I thought it important to write items that reflected only the most commonly discussed dimensions to include in the pilot test. I reasoned that a pilot test of the key features would be the best test of a test; if this test proved reliable then I could proceed with testing all the dimensions of insight. These features were as follows: action, whole self, new understanding, peace, interpreting device, perspective, expansive knowledge, dissonance, part of personal history, and confrontation. (I added two of my own hunches, sharing insight and the presence of insight, only to find them miserably unsupported.) Several examples are shown in Table 4.1 (the final versions of the test appear later in the chapter).

During the spring semester of 1986, 94 students took the 30-item pilot test that asked them to report their experience of writing expressive essays for their first-year composition class. The internal consistency or reliability of this pilot test can now be discussed.

Each item had five responses from which a person could choose (*strongly agree* to *strongly disagree*), and each of these responses corresponded to a number from 1 to 5. A test constructor must cast a few of the items in negative terms so as to avoid the yay-saying phenomenon; these items must be recoded before performing any statistical analyses. Because students used computer-scored sheets, recoding was an easy task. I employed the reliability program from SPSSX to calculate a reliability figure.

For the sake of illustration, imagine reliability as a voting

Table 4.1. Sample Items of Insight Test

Dimension	Sample Item
Dissonance	This was a topic that I was curious about.
Action	I am ready to act on what I learned in this essay.
Expansive Understanding	I keep thinking about what I learned in this essay.

constituency: The more votes in common, the more powerful the group. Similarly, the more items measuring the same thing, the more reliable (and powerful) the test. Reliability calculations compare each item to the total score of all test takers; what is reported is the degree to which each item contributed to that total. In practical terms, this figure is reported in terms of a number from 0.0 to 1.0. A reliability figure of above .60, for exploratory work, is considered encouraging. For more advanced work, a reliability figure of .70 and preferably higher is expected.

For this pilot test, the internal consistency measure, Cronbach's alpha, was .84, indicating a high degree of precision of measurement and a high degree of unity in what the items were measuring. The success of this pilot measure led me to believe that insight could be measured as it is described by experts in a variety of fields; it also led me to believe that the Likert-type format was the appropriate one for this venture.

CREATING AN ITEM POOL

As is commonly known, the Scholastic Assessment Tests (SAT) are really a subset of an enormous pool of items. There are computer files at Educational Testing Service (ETS) filled with literally thousands and thousands of sample questions. This year's SAT test is but a small set of those items. The next stage in test construction is to model that procedure: The researcher must compose a domain of *items* from which to draw sample tests. This procedure enables researchers to perfect the items regarding wording and content. That is, keeping records of how the items themselves individually measure the construct (each one gets rated individually) helps perfect the test as a whole. Such procedures enable researchers to develop reliable and valid tests for the construct.

How many should be developed? This question is not answered in strictly mathematical terms but rather is answered regarding the population who will take the test. A large number of people representative of those to whom the final test will be given should take a large number of items: Nunnally advised that 300 to 1,000 persons should take each item and that ideally, a 5:1 subject:item ratio should obtain. Imagine the results if only 50 people responded to a question as opposed to 500 answering it; the statistical clarity regarding how well that item functions in a reliable test is ever so much more enhanced in the latter case.

At the time, which was fall semester of 1986, I had articulated 14 of the 16 dimensions of insight: Results from the sub-sequent item pool made me separate two more from the original 14 to make 16 (for clarity). In any case, I decided that 10 questions for each of 14 items were sufficient in terms of what was needed to study the items and what was possible for students to answer given 1 hour of class time. Therefore, the item pool consisted of 140 items. Fellow graduate students and I wrote them.

The group to whom this test was aimed was college-level writers, thus I asked fellow teaching assistants at a large midwestern university to offer one entire class period in which to test the item pool. The number of subjects taking the large item pool was 627; the number dropped to 566 after missing cases were found in the statistical analysis. Nevertheless, this number almost reaches the 5:1 ratio, which would have been 700. As participation was voluntary, no more subjects were available. Because this large sample size offsets much error, the results can be considered reliable despite the miss of the 5:1 ratio.

Once the large group of students took the 140-item test, attention shifts to the items, each of which has 566 responses that, as a group, are analyzed for reliability. Two analyses are performed: percentage responses and item-total correlations. The first is an almost visual check that the range that the Likert-type item affords is really being used. The second is a numerical procedure that assigns a number to the degree of relatedness each item has to the total score.

Percentage Responses

An initial analysis of items determines how spread out the responses are among the various choices. Imagine that a fourth- grade class was given a multiple-choice item and that the item had four possible responses, letters A through D. If everyone circled letter b, the test is not doing what a test should do, namely, discriminate. A test's function is to discriminate among its takers; if it does not, it is not really testing them. (One exception to this general rule is when very savvy students take an exam—then the items must be made even more difficult to ensure discrimination.) What test constructors look for is a response pattern that shows that each of the four responses attracts some respondents. The test-scoring center usually issues such percentage response figures with reports of scores.

On a Likert-type test, students do not all answer the letter b, but the scoring patterns can be just as lopsided. For instance, on one item students can all answer *agree* or *strongly agree* and in such cases the item is not discriminating. (One exception to this general rule is that when testing for a new construct, some researchers add questions that only a few very people can answer correctly in terms of the construct, just to test the test.)

I decided to discard an item if the responses to the two high or low alternatives combined (e.g., *agree* plus *strongly agree*, or, *disagree* plus *strongly disagree*) exceeded 80%. Fortunately, none had to be discarded on this basis because so few items had percentage response rates over 80% for the combined alternatives. Neither did items show 80% at the middle response. If a researcher has to reconsider items because of percentage response rate, other item writers may help in rewording or reshaping the items.

Item-Total Correlations

The most important test of test items is this mathematical procedure. It correlates each item with the total test score. That is, the computer has the listings of how each of the 566 students responded to all 140 items. It also has the sum total of how all 566 students did on the test as a whole. Imagine the computer separating Item 58 and isolating the scores on it from all the other items. Here is Item 58:

"I see my subject in a new light now."

The reliability program on SPSSX prints out how each item fared, that is, how well it contributed to the total test score. If Item 58 was in sync with the construct of insight, measuring what aspect of insight it was supposed to, then the numerical analysis of how well it supported the total test score would be high. In terms of rating such a quality, the numbers range from 0.0 to 1.0, *not correlated* to *fully correlated*. But how high is high?

Nunnally recommended making such decisions according to the summary chart shown in Table 4.2.

Any item that has a zero as a score shows that it has no measurement power, so to speak, regarding the construct at hand. Thus it is discarded. Low negative correlations are worse than zero correlations because they are not only unrelated, they are a weak and poor relation, so those are discarded too. It might seem odd that the very highly negatively correlated items are not discarded, ones for instance that have a score of -.7. Such a score might seem of no value, yet it can be very helpful. That item is measuring very well, therefore it is recoded; that is, the wording

Table 4.2. How to Interpret Correlation Figures

Correlation	Decision
High positive (+1 to .3)	Retain
Low positive (.3 to 0)	Consider
Zero	Discard
Low negative (0 to -.3)	Discard
High negative (-.3 to -1)	Recode

is kept, but the score inverted. Naturally, those items with high positive correlations are retained. For the sake of illustration, next are a few samples of each.

Item 58 scored .5477 which, according to Table 4.2, is good; the item was therefore retained. Because this item pool had so many good items, I decided to set the limit on high positive correlations at .4 rather than at .3. Another case is Item 27. This item received -.1645:

"I still see many ways to explain my subject."

This item was discarded. It is a negatively worded item (one that needs to be recoded); its wording may be unclear and ambiguous possibly because the two verbs (see and explain) do not work well together.

The following is a zero correlation, Item 80, which received a score of -.0092:

"This essay unearthed more questions than it did answers."

This is another negatively worded item. Perhaps the word unearthed was confusing.

To conclude these illustrations, Item 50 has a high negative correlation. Item 50 had a score of -.4234:

"I learned a lot, but I know I have more to understand."

This item refers to the feature of having the limits of one's knowledge exposed. This item could have been retained, but because there were so many items with high positive correlations, and many with correlations above .4, this one was set aside.

I retained 69 of the original 140 items and discarded 71. These 69 compose the pool out of which I can draw sample tests. Usually 30 items are needed to compose a test of high reliability, high meaning above .80. The 69 items available will support two separate tests of 30 items each. If, upon further testing of these sample tests of 30 items each, these new tests do not have a high enough reliability, the advice given is to add items 5 or 10 at a time and estimate the reliability. But this is the next project to be discussed, and before so doing, some of the theoretical or validity issues that surfaced from the results of the item pool need discussion.

Subsets of the Item Pool

Something in which many researchers might be interested is how the features of insight fared as measurement instruments in themselves. That is, when features of insight are separated into mini-tests (about 10 items each), how well does each measure? Table 4.3 outlines the reliabilities that each of the features or dimensions of insight received.

Table 4.3. Dimension Reliabilities in Descending Order

Dimension	Cronbach's Alpha
Whole self	(.9307)
Interpreting device	(.8330)
Accepting atmosphere	(.8308)
Action	(.8300)
Expansive understanding	(.8288)
Part of personal history	(.7911)
Dissonance	(.7742)
New understanding	(.7390)
Perspective shift	(.7112)
New vision	(.6961)
Peace	(.6568)
Limits of knowledge	(.6389)
Confrontation	(.6155)
Permanently true	(.6050)
Simple problem resolution	(.3011)
Needs testing	(.1446)

The feature of whole self is the one that measures insight the best. In fact, all the dimensions except for "Simple problem resolution" and "Needs testing" contribute very well to the over-all test. I have yet to figure out why these two are such poor measurement instruments. This regrouping of items into their respective dimensions also enhances the validity because we see that these items are working together to measure insight well. Tests could be developed from these subsets, and, in fact, the SAT and most tests of that nature have subsets that are treated in this way. But for now, let us return to the task at hand, developing an insight test to be used by college instructors in conjunction with a writing assignment.

Overall Reliability Figure for the Item Pool

The most important number in this entire chapter is the following one: .9652. This number is the overall reliability figure (Cronbach's alpha) for the item pool, and it is very high. This figure indicates that the item pool is a good test: It is reliable and its items measure in unison. It also means that tests taken as samples from appropriate items from the pool will be reliable ones. Some researchers say that Likert-type item pools yield high reliability figures, but even so, this one is very high indicating the strength of its items. High internal consistency cannot result without these items measuring in unison.

COMPOSING ALTERNATE FORMS OF THE INSIGHT TEST

Taking the 69 items that have item-total correlations above the .4 mark, I sorted the items by dimension and composed parallel tests. These parallel tests each have a reliability figure of .94 (Cronbach's alpha). Alternative forms are important because they assure us that the domain can be defined well enough to support separate exams (Nunnally, 1978, p. 232). The reliability figure for both tests is high enough with 30 items; nevertheless, if the reliability figure is not as high as desired, researchers are told to add more items until the desired figure is gained.

A further test of the construct regarding matters of time can be conducted with alternative forms. Ideally, I should have a large group of people (at least 300) take these tests about 2 weeks apart. This time period allows variations in ability and attitude to occur (Nunnally, 1978, p. 230). If the correlation between the two exams is markedly lower than the alpha for each of the exams (.94 in this case), then the construct is said to be influenced by large variations in people over short periods of time (Nunnally, 1978, p. 230). Certain kinds of tests (of moods or attitudes especially) are subject to special investigations regarding alternative forms because people do vary widely over short periods of time regarding the subject matter. I have not had sufficient numbers of students yet to make such investigations regarding insight.

DURATION AND TEST ADMINISTRATION DETAILS

Either form of the insight test should take about 15 minutes to complete (see Tables 4.4 and 4.5). This test can be easily administered during class time. Although the tests can be taken at home, so many variations are present in the individual environments that they can distort the overall information about the class; if, however, a more individual and descriptive report is desired, such application is fine. In such cases, professors may wish students to respond in prose to anything that the questionnaire fosters. If given in class, the teacher should read aloud the directions that appear at the top of either form. These directions lead students away from connecting their writing experience with grades. As most readers are probably aware, research policy regarding subjects is that as much as possible is to be shared with students; therefore, teachers may wish to tell them exactly why this information is desired (i.e., to improve teaching and learning) without unduly leading (and misleading) students by using the term *insight*.

One important point needs to be clarified: This test is connected with one writing assignment, not a semester's worth of assignments. That is, this test cannot establish that one's method of teaching throughout a semester produces more insight than another method; it can only relate students' experiences with one writing task. Insight is a fundamentally context-grounded event: We do not have insights in general, we have them with particular questions in particular settings. Therefore, please make no mistake: This test corresponds only to one writing event.

Table 4.4. Insight Test: Form A

Thank you for volunteering to take this test. Your responses will eventually help us improve English 101. Instructions:

1. Recall the subject and content of your essay. What it meant to you is the subject of this exam—so think about what it meant to you.

2. Answer the following questions using the grid sheet for your responses. The usual number 2 lead pencil is needed.

3. Don't worry about how "good" your essay was. All that's important is how much you got out of it. If you didn't get much out of it, please say so. This test isn't related to your grades at all.

4. There are no right or wrong answers. Please be *totally* honest.

A	B	C	D	E
STRONGLY DISAGREE	DISAGREE	NEUTRAL	AGREE	STRONGLY AGREE

1. I am ready to act on what I learned in this essay.

2. I reached a very sharp understanding of my subject.

3. I don't want to think about this subject anymore.

4. I've used or will use my essay or the contents of it for some purpose other than just sharing my thoughts.

5. Writing this time touched me.

6. I can reflect on my previous way of understanding this topic thanks to this essay.

7. This essay doesn't relate to my life.

8. I feel a great sense of peace after writing about this topic.

9. This was a topic that I was curious about.

10. I'm glad I could write about this topic to understand it better.

11. This paper helped me put things in perspective.

12. Writing helped me see how to handle something in my life.

13. After writing about this topic I understand it more clearly.

Table 4.4. Insight Test: Form A (cont.)

14. I keep thinking about what I learned in this essay.

15. No one would benefit from reading this, even me.

16. I was so caught up in writing this paper.

17. During my writing I realized how much I knew and how much I didn't know.

18. Writing about this topic helps me in day-to-day living.

19. I feel refreshed after writing this essay.

20. I didn't care about this essay topic at all.

21. I was ready and willing to explore this topic.

22. My way of seeing the subject is the same now as before writing.

23. After writing this essay I see a course of action.

24. I really didn't know what I was talking about in this essay.

25. I'd like to forget that I ever wrote this paper.

26. Certain things in the past are clearer now that I've written on this topic.

27. I just wrote this paper as an assignment, it didn't do anything for me.

28. I couldn't care less about this topic.

29. I didn't learn anything while writing this assignment.

30. This essay doesn't mean anything to me.

Table 4.5. Insight Test: Form B

Thank you for volunteering to take this test. Your responses will eventually help us improve English 101. Instructions:

1. Recall the subject and content of your essay. What it meant to you is the subject of this exam—so think about what it meant to you.

2. Answer the following questions using the grid sheet for your responses. The usual number 2 lead pencil is needed.

3. Don't worry about how "good" your essay was. All that's important is how much you got out of it. If you didn't get much out of it, please say so. This test isn't related to your grades at all.

4. There are no right or wrong answers. Please be totally honest.

A	B	C	D	E
STRONGLY DISAGREE	DISAGREE	NEUTRAL	AGREE	STRONGLY AGREE

1. I'd like to put into action something I now understand thanks to writing.

2. I reached a totally new understanding of this subject.

3. I don't want to review the contents of this essay ever again.

4. I want to share my thoughts on this matter to help other people.

5. A lot of heart went into this paper.

6. My understanding lit up new paths for me to explore.

7. I'd like to bury this paper in the backyard.

8. I feel a special calmness after writing this essay.

9. I felt curious about this subject before writing.

10. Writing gave me a chance to struggle with questions I've had about this subject.

11. I see my subject in a new light now.

12. I've made a decision to act differently thanks to writing this essay.

13. I understand what is at the heart of my topic.

Table 4.5. Insight Test: Form B (cont.)

---

14. The subject keeps growing in my mind.
15. My essay is worthless.
16. I found my whole self involved in this essay.
17. I see clearly the difference between what I knew before I wrote and what I know now.
18. This essay is now part of my life.
19. I feel powerful and happy with the results of my writing.
20. My heart wasn't in this paper at all.
21. I didn't adequately explore my topic.
22. New worlds opened up for me while writing this essay.
23. This essay doesn't inspire me to do anything.
24. Writing about this topic clarified my ideas.
25. I can't see myself ever forgetting what I wrote about.
26. I'd never use what I wrote about for anything.
27. I didn't get much out of writing this essay.
28. I didn't get involved in this assignment.
29. I know about the same now as I did when I wrote the paper.
30. I can hardly remember what I wrote about.

SCORING PROCEDURES

Scoring this test is very simple. One set of class scores can be done by hand in an hour at most, but using computer-scored answer sheets facilitates scoring, especially for large numbers of students. Computer-scored sheets also enable teachers and researchers to compare scores more easily across years or semesters or between assignments or pedagogies. In order to begin scoring, the negatively worded items that appear below must be recoded. To recode an item means to assign the opposite value to that question. Positively worded items would be scored as follows:

strongly agree = 5
agree = 4
neutral = 3
disagree = 2
strongly disagree = 1

When students report *strongly agree* to a negatively worded question, they are really reporting a very negative experience and should receive the opposite score: 5s should be 1s, 4s should be 2s, 2s should be 4s, and 1s should be 5s (see Table 4.6).

Once these items have received their proper scores, the total can be calculated. Table 4.7 indicates how to interpret the totals. Students reporting a score in the first category of Table 4.7 have consistently reported having had an insight experience—confronting a personally meaningful dissonance with their whole self

Table 4.6. Items to be Recoded from Forms A and B

Form A	Form B
3	3
7	7
1 5	1 5
2 0	2 0
2 2	2 1
2 4	2 3
2 5	2 6
2 7	2 7
2 8	2 8
2 9	2 9
3 0	3 0

Table 4.7. Interpreting Total Insight Test Scores

Writing This Assignment Yielded	Total Test Scores
An insight experience	150 - 127
Increased understanding	126 - 103
Negligible effect on understanding	102 - 77
Negative effect on understanding	78 - 55
Frustration, confusion, isolation	54 - 30

and coming to a simple solution that affords them peace, direction, continued use of the discovery, and other benefits described in Chapter 2.

It is conceivable that students might not reach insight but would improve their understanding, and this is the second category shown in Table 4.7. Students with what psychologists would call "intellectual" insight might have truly engaged themselves in confronting a personal dissonance but did not reach a simple solution. They would mark this test in such a way that they would agree with the involvement and dissonance items but disagree with those regarding the qualities and benefits of insight.

Students who marked mostly the *neutral* response are indicating that writing did not touch them personally nor did it enhance their understanding of the topic.

Students who marked the *disagree* response predominantly are indicating some frustration and confusion either with the assignment or with their understanding of the topic.

Those students who score in the last category in the table are reporting a very negative experience with writing. They are hostile, confused, and frustrated. It is important to consider some reasons why this experience might occur.

One must ascertain, in these two latter categories, how much students were asked, encouraged, and actually assigned to engage in a meaningful personal dissonance. If students did not know that this was the goal of the assignment, it would be unfair to assume that the students did not want to engage themselves. (The next chapter contains suggestions about incorporating such assignments into teaching, no matter which discipline.) Discussions I have had with students who have reported very negative experiences regarding writing indicate that they were very frustrated with the assignment, did not understand what was being asked of them, and chose not to engage themselves personally.

These latter categories should be the subject of further research. The efforts in this study have been directed more toward the insight experience rather than its opposite; nevertheless, understanding these experiences would be of great importance to teaching, writing research, and learning studies.

Two writers give us a glimpse into these latter categories. Lonergan (1957/1978) said that the flight from insight produces isolation; this isolation is not only from self but from those (e.g., class members, professors, student's friends) who would profit from the attempt at insight. Finley (1978), working on what insight meant to Merton, said that insight was a genuine communion. Regarding our students reporting very negative experiences, Finley's words may help explain this situation: "The failure to communicate is frustration. The failure to commune is despair" (p. 123). The reasons for frustration and despair, I suspect, are rich and complex—a very worthy project for which this test can be used.

These scores should never be used to grade students on their progress in a class, no matter how much the instructor wants insight. Insight does not come when called, it cannot be summoned at will. Therefore, it is not fair to expect that students should have insight to get a high grade. Sometimes confusion readies us for insight; that is, a student who expresses confusion might really be seeing the larger picture and eventually resolves the dissonance. This test should make teachers aware of how students are understanding the task at hand and the subject matter. It should not be used to penalize someone for not having insight. Now some of the final issues in test construction are considered.

NORMS

Nunnally (1978) broadly defined *norms* as "any scores that provide a frame of reference for interpreting the scores of particular persons" (p. 264). Although necessary for any national achievement test, they are not essential for achievement tests used in educational experiments (p. 265). To present them, researchers must test thousands of students from various parts of the country and offer these scores in percentile form. Because this test is to be used in educational research and not nationally, norms will not be presented for it.

TEST VALIDATION

The final considerations in test construction are whether the test actually measures what it purports to measure and what scores from it mean in a theoretical and practical sense.

Construct Validity

A *construct* is a label for a set of symptoms or phenomena. The goal of the test constructor, at the end of the process of composing a test, is to establish that this newly composed test does not in fact duplicate what another already existing test could provide. A test constructor's worst fears are that the construct really does not exist but can be called by another name.

Psychologists number about 400 constructs, of which there are tests for some, such as anxiety, depression, and so forth. In writing research, we have yet to empirically validate many of our new labels for writing phenomena. The Daly-Miller (1985) test for writing apprehension is a good example of a test for a construct in writing research. The issue now is how to ascertain that this test for insight in writing measures what it says it does

Many researchers today (Cronbach, 1988; Geisinger, 1992; Messick, 1989) say that it is impossible to ever know conclusively that a valid test has been created. How does one approximate such knowledge? By a long series of comparisons, say psychometricians, of the new test to tests of similar and dissimilar constructs. The reasoning goes as follows: Tests of similar constructs should have positive but not perfect correlations. If the two constructs are related theoretically, but are truly distinct constructs or sets of phenomena, then the correlations between tests for these two constructs should reveal their similarity but not be so high as to intuit that they are identical constructs. The same reasoning holds for dissimilar ones: Tests of dissimilar constructs should not be correlated. Such testing takes years because in each instance the researcher needs a large number of people to take both tests. In educational work, this is not always easy: Securing the numbers of students and justifying the need for giving students what appear to be a series of meaningless and unrelated exams is difficult.

Nevertheless, I began such work on a relatively small set of students ($n = 217$) at a small college. The students were enrolled in a General Education class that was a requirement for all first-year students. With the mandate that the rhetoric department was to assess the writing situation at the college, I was given permission to give the Insight Test, a creativity test, and a memory test to as many students as volunteered.

The Creativity Checklist (Johnson, 1979) is a series of qualities or characteristics (e.g., "observed flexibility," "observed preference for complexity") that teachers were asked to rate for each of the students in their classroom. Johnson said "creativity appears as an unexpected, positive self-referenced, or productive act emitted spontaneously by a person within a social interaction setting. The Creativity Checklist focuses our attention on those elements implicated in creative expression" (p. 1). It is based on the creativity research of Torrance (1970).

I posed creativity as a similar construct to insight, but not equal to it. It is possible, for instance, to be creative in the larger or more general sense of the word (e.g., in serving dinner tonight), but not insightful, which is a more specific form of creativity. The comparison of scores revealed as much: The degree of relatedness was zero with no significance (r = .0384, p = .287). (Not all teachers, interestingly, used the full range of the scale: Only the professors in the humanities displayed full-range scores, whereas some professors, in political science for instance, used far fewer gradations. Perhaps training the professors would yield a higher degree of relatedness of the two constructs.)

I devised the test of memory because no established test existed that corresponded to the writing task. In theory, one does not forget an insight—it has tremendous value for the future as well as for the present. Students were asked to comment on how well they remembered what they wrote; I tallied responses by assigning a high score to those responses that indicated both memory and articulation of the substance of the essay. Low scores were given to responses that indicated no memory of what the student wrote or learned (e.g., one student wrote "I don't recall what I wrote about even though it's under my chair"). In the comparison of scores, insight and memory had a low positive correlation (r = .1852) that is significant (p = .003).

These two efforts at construct validity are hopeful: They clearly say that the construct of insight cannot be duplicated in testing using creativity or memory tests. Tests of dissimilar constructs (e.g., anxiety) are in order.

Relevance/Utility

Relevance/utility refers to the match between the content of the test and the form of the test. The Insight Test has relevance/utility because it is meaningful to speak of degrees of insight or degrees of the resolution of dissonance; the form of the test—the Likert-type items—match this kind of experience. It also has relevance/utility by being a self-report that respects the quality and individuality of the insight experience. The test does not rate anyone's insights, it merely presents students' own admissions that they have occurred.

Value Implications

Value implications have three aspects, according to Messick (1988):

> The consequential basis of test interpretation is the appraisal of the value implications of the construct label, of the theory underlying test interpretation, and of the ideologies in which the theory is embedded. A central issue is whether or not the theoretical implications and the value implications of the test interpretation are not ancillary, but, rather, integral to score meaning. (p. 20)

Let us appraise each of these three things separately. The "value implications of the construct label" refer to what it means when a student receives a score on the Insight Test. A value is an amount equivalent for something else; a high score on the Insight Test is equivalent for the resolution of a complex and meaningful dissonance with the full person. This label is quite valuable for educational purposes. For so long we have been without any way to describe or identify that which so many teachers, both of writing and of many other disciplines, have as the goal of writing. Second, the theory that undergirds test interpretation can be appraised as valuable too. It claims that it is possible and meaningful or important to distinguish among students who have had an insight, those who have not, and those in between. That is, this theory more generally states that it is possible and meaningful to assign a score to real events. Because the theory of test interpretation and the value implications follow the nature of the insight experience, they are integral (and not ancillary) to score meaning.

The ideologies in which the theory is embedded point to the reductionist and empirical claims that it is possible to split up or analyze experiences and give numbers to the parts. It is this ideology that has, in fact, prevented serious inquiry of non-rational subjects like insight, premonition, or intuition to give several examples. These subjects cannot be grasped or summoned to be analyzed. It is this ideology that has also limited the ways that our culture looks at writing, which, too, is seen as mysterious and not lending itself readily to analysis.

When students respond to items on the Insight Test, they are not analyzing their insights: They are analyzing their experience of writing in light of the possibility (or lack) of the insight experience. It is meaningful and valid to speak of gradations of an experience, while it is not meaningful to ask students to rate, if you will, their insights in and of themselves. A comparison: Imagine 20 people see the movie *Sleepless in Seattle* and someone asks each of them how moved they were by that film. How deeply (if at all) they were moved by the film can be described using a range of responses; nevertheless, what cannot be described using a range of responses is why and how they were (or were not) moved. Thus, the ideologies that foster analytical description do work for the self-report of an insight experience after writing.

Where such ideologies have caused problems in English is in the traditional tests of grammar that substitute for writing exams. These tests are used to further those students who wish success in conforming to a competitive, consumer society. Berlin (1984) wrote that in the writing classroom the loss of the richness of classical rhetoric for the emphasis on grammatical correctness "encourages a mode of behavior that helps students in their move up the corporate ladder—correctness in usage, grammar, clothing, thought, and a certain sterile objectivity and disinterestedness" (p. 75). To test for insight signals an interest in the individuality and whole person of each of our students.

Bellah, Madsen, Sullivan, Swidler, and Tipton (1991), in their book *The Good Society*, claimed that there is great value in reversing the trend in education away from utilitarian individualism (which the exclusive emphasis on grammatical correctness fosters) and toward the integration of the whole person. They wrote:

> We must recover an enlarged paradigm of knowledge, which recognizes the value of science but acknowledges that other ways of knowing have equal dignity. Practical reason, in its classical sense of moral reason, must regain its importance in our educational life. We must give more than a token bow to art and literature as mere vessels of expressive values, for they can often give us deep moral insight. Ethos is the very subject matter of the humanities and social sciences. . . . (p. 177)

In writing classrooms, perhaps as in few others, students can exercise alternate ways of knowing and display ethos and moral reasoning. When the wisdom and insight that minority students can bring to such classrooms is present, even greater insight for the group is possible. Bellah et al. wrote that "It is clearly time to reintegrate cognition with a more fully human understanding" (p. 178). The Insight Test has such integration as its goal.

Social Consequences

Messick (1989) wrote that the "consequential basis of test interpretation is the appraisal of both potential and actual social consequences of the applied setting" (p. 20). An intended social consequence is the emphasis on insight in the writing situations of college students.

In actual settings, I have found the following consequences: The test enables teachers to identify and dialogue with students about their insights (or lack of), and it enables writing professors to dialogue with professors in other disciplines about pedagogical goals beyond grammatical correctness and stylistic elegance. Potential dangers would occur if insight scores were in some way connected to a student's grade or if insight scores were connected to a teacher's performance.

CONCLUSION

This chapter presented the development of a test for insight as a result of writing. The methodology for the design of the test comes from Nunnally's (1978) *Psychometric Theory* and is augmented by the work of Geisinger (1992) and Messick (1988). Even for readers unfamiliar with statistics, such ventures into test construction are possible with consultants from educational psychology.

5

Fostering Insight in College Writing

Tillich (1951) stressed that insight was never abstract or independent: As Dulles (1985) explained, "it is always correlated with human questions arising out of a specific cultural and historical context" (p. 102). This chapter presents ways of creating situations of human questioning to enhance the insight process. In fact, if one word could summarize this chapter, it would be *space.* The teacher needs to give students space to have insight; the classroom must be a space of questioning; students needs to realize their own space that makes them question.

The suggestions in this chapter are to be broadly interpreted, not to be seen as set guidelines. To be interested in insight is to be interested in the individual in all his or her rich heritage, and clearly teachers know best how to accomplish the overall goals proposed in order that their students become wonderers. The general goal for creating the context for insight is to elicit from students the preconditions of insight: dissonance and whole-personed confrontation. Conversely, what should be eliminated from teaching and assignments is anything that anesthetizes, pacifies, or inhibits. Condescending, domineering, authoritarian behavior cannot foster insight in the classroom and neither can assignments that smack of it. Rather, with discretion, reserve, and respect, professors should consider students as similar to themselves—persons who never pick up a book without a question to be answered and who are probably professors because they so frequently question and confront.

CREATING DISSONANCE AND WHOLE-PERSONED CONFRONTATION IN THE CLASSROOM AND BEYOND

Let us follow the average professor and class as they run the course of a semester in order to insert dissonance and confrontation before the assigned paper is collected.

Reading Assignments

Most courses require reading that is done alone and tested perhaps weeks after the reading. Although this method promotes independence (and ingenuity for students who find both reading and finding a place to read troublesome), it does not promote dissonance. Dissonance will only occur in this model when students are moved by the material. Students may understand reading to be a matter of absorbing material rather than as the interactive process that modern psycholinguistics and literary scholars describe it to be. The following suggestions are offered to circumvent these problems and to create a climate of dissonance and confrontation:

1. The professor must select books that he or she finds puzzling and interesting so that he or she reflects the kind of enthusiasm he or she wishes students to have and so that the professor she poses appropriate questions.
2. A journal should be kept wherein students respond to readings personally without concern for proof, explanation, or mechanical correctness. Entries can be read aloud to direct attention to those students who were uninhibited about their responses and to those who confronted dissonances.
3. Quick feedback on how students understand the readings can be gained through collecting index cards with their ideas.

4. Short, easily graded quizzes assure professors of students' progress and understanding (this step avoids making essays bear the burden of being a test).
5. Collaborative groups that help students discuss their personal reactions to the readings should be formed (to save class time, these groups can be assigned to meet outside of class; the group can present a log of activities to assure the professor of their work).

These reading assignments should encourage students to respond personally to the material; they should also assure the professor that they have read and understood it.

Classroom Interactions

The interaction between the professor and the students and among students themselves sets the tone for how much real questioning and confronting can go on. The lecture format that predominates in college classrooms can promote passivity and, if fact-based, can give the impression that human questioning was never the genesis of the material.

In order to create the context of insight in the classroom itself, the following are some suggestions:

1. There should be a welcoming atmosphere for students' ideas so that students know professors understand them (or try to).
2. The professor should ask sincere questions that demonstrate his or her desire for students' opinions.
3. There should be direct confrontation of the previous kinds of relationships students have had with teachers. A discussion should be held of what the traditional roles of "teacher" and "student" feel like and how viable they are for growth in writing. The group should work to define the ideal working relationship.
4. Environmental instruction (Hillocks, 1984) that involves students directly in what they are to learn is recommended.
5. Students need to hear from their professor that repeating ideas given in lectures is not desired; students need to indicate in written essays that they have gone beyond the class lectures.

When students feel understood and welcomed, then real learning takes place; they are not hiding their real thoughts or trying to please the teacher. It takes much courage and patience to listen, especially when students mouth ideas that cause others so much pain (imagine Marvin who said that businesses really do have to exploit Third World countries to get ahead, Andy who wrote about how to avoid seeing the poverty while on vacation on an exotic French island, and Michelle who thought illiterates should never have children). It is when such ideas are brought out, however, that comparison can begin. Rokeach (1979) said that long-term value change comes not through teaching values, but through the comparison of values. Change comes about when a person considers his or her own values deficient in comparison to another's stronger or better values; the direction is there and so is the desire.

Writing Assignments

The key to providing a context for dissonance and confrontation (and better writing) is in planning exercises and multiple drafts. The planning exercises increase the quality of thought for the essay, and the multiple drafts increase the quality of prose (and thinking, too). The reason professors receive wretched prose is because students have not been forced to consider the professor's and their own questions in sufficient depth; furthermore, they often execute one version at the last possible moment. All of this spells despair for teachers when reading their papers.

The pedagogy referred to here can be found in greater detail in Lauer et al. (1991), *Four Worlds of Writing*. The adaptations are designed to make this pedagogy more generally applicable to the average college course. A student example of some of these steps follows. Here are the suggestions:

1. Ask students to write a list of what puzzles them about the book they are reading. Draw on emotions they have toward the subject: anger, confusion, recurring thoughts, excitement, a willingness to forget about certain sections, and so forth.
2. Have students contrast their expectations and values with what they are learning.
3. Ask students to form a question that embodies what they need to know to resolve their puzzlement. Have them write five questions to clarify the wording. Teachers can

assess the questions on two points: Questions should point to the book (not to further research beyond the scope of the class), and they should be intellectually responsible.

4. Have students explore their question by requesting three pages of relevant quotes from the book along with the student's attitude next to the quote (this exercise forces close reading and fosters good development in the final version). Have students consider their subject from various perspectives using the tagmemic heuristic procedure that considers subjects from three perspectives (not just one): static, dynamic (in process and change), and relative (in relation to other similar and dissimilar subjects).

5. Incubation follows exploration, meaning that no conscious work should be done on the project for at least one night. Exploration entails much work and the rest is needed.

6. Tell students to answer the question they posed in one sentence. Have them write five versions of the answer until the wording is clear. This one sentence answer will become the thesis or focus of the essay.

7. The first version of the essay unwraps the focus for the writer alone. Tell students that this is their chance to really write and to write it for themselves in their own voice. Other drafts will be audience-centered. The first version is an ideas draft without concern for style, grammar, or audience.

8. Have peer groups read the first version for the focus alone and suggest means of developing and organizing the essay for the appropriate audience.

9. Praise clear focuses and movements in thinking aloud in class.

10. Provide a model of the assignment (preferably one written by the professor him- or herself or by previous students).

11. The second version should be a more formal draft with concern for development, organization, style, and mechanics.

12. Peer groups should review the second version and make specific suggestions.

13. Bring in copies of papers or sections of papers that are well written. Praise strong efforts regarding insight and good writing.

14. Conferences with the professor should be planned, if possible after the second version and peer group meetings.
Advise students to ask their own questions regarding the
improvement of their draft before adding comments.

The number of reading assignments and the reading load
for the instructor can seem overwhelming. A periodic fast check
of students' progress on questions, focuses, essay development,
organization, and revision goals can be had through the collection
of index cards. A brief statement of where students are in their
writing process will help teachers keep a record without having
to read everything. Another idea to cut the reading load is to assign
stages of work to be reviewed by peer groups held outside class.
Students can submit a group log to indicate attendance and
progress. The simplest check would be to credit in class those
students who have completed a preliminary task, such as a first
version, without reading it. The overall idea is to structure a
sequence of reading and writing assignments that promote reflection through dissonance and exploration.
    Grading or crediting everything students do, from planning
exercises to peer responses (which are written) to group logs,
saves these exercises from being perceived as perfunctory when
in fact they model actual writing and business practices in text
construction. Keeping these exercises and drafts in a portfolio is
an option that allows the instructor to evaluate student work when
convenient and in a focused way.

STUDENT MODEL OF WRITING EXERCISES

The sample of student writing that follows comes from a student
enrolled in a composition course for first-year students called
Writers Seminar. The goal of the course is to prepare students for
academic writing they will face in subsequent college courses.
During the last 3 weeks, the class read Sallie McFague's (1987)
Models of God in order to watch an academic person construct an
argument and respond to it. In a nutshell, McFague argued against
paternal and imperialist images of God and proposed the
metaphors of mother, lover, and friend as more conducive to the
values of concern, respect, and mutuality that are needed in this
age of environmental threats. I wanted to read this book myself for
several reasons: As a scholar I find that theology (and literature)
allow or discuss the fullest existence of the human person and that

this perspective is terrifically valuable and needed today; I found McFague's book exciting for its integration of masculine and feminine qualities of God; as a professor I thought McFague's argument structure was interesting (and somewhat flawed) and would provoke discussion; and I had had the book recommended as important and popular. I was taking a course in theology at the time that enabled me to explain enough history to make the book intelligible to my students. The assignment was to produce a three- to five-page paper that showed an understanding of the book and its basic tenets along with an answer to a question that the student posed.

As a teacher, I reasoned that if I picked a theology book in order to practice academic writing, the arguments would be obvious because they were so foreign to most of my students. I thought that arguing about theology would help them see how academics work. The course evaluations said as much.

In order to get the most out of this example, keep in mind what a typical assignment might be and contrast that with the following student's work. Typically, students are asked to produce only one draft of a report on a book without any planning exercises. Here, Doris is asked to compose a paper in a series of stages.

Dissonance

Students are asked to contrast their values and expectations with what McFague presented. Doris expresses her dissonance in the following section:

> My Values and Expectations versus The Book's
>
> I always thought that religion wanted us to view God in one certain way. But the book widens our perspectives on how to view God and challenges traditional ways we see God.
>
> God seemed to be thought of in special times, good times and bad. But in the book immanence is universal—that it is not limited to special times.
>
> I never thought of the world as God's body. The book suggests that if we see the world as God's body we will indeed know we tread on sacred ground.
>
> I thought that this book would be boring because I'm not a religious person. The book is interesting because it looks at God differently and puts this thinking in relationship to modern times.

Students are then asked to form a question that embodies their dissonance.

> Doris' question: "Why is the model of God as Friend an important metaphor?"

Her question shows her particular fascination with one aspect of McFague's text. I approved this question because it would easily support a three-to five-page essay.

Exploration

In the next stage students were asked to complete an exploration of their question. The tagmemic heuristic is employed. What follows is Doris' exploration; it is rich and well done.

Static View

> Through the ages most religious have looked upon God as our all-powerful savior. The metaphors of God are seen in many images—"As king, ruler, lord, master, and governor, and the concepts that accompany them of God as absolute, complete, transcendent, and omnipotent . . . " (p. 19). God is traditionally seen as male. The God-world relationship is one in which God is "externally related to the world as the power that totally controls it" (p. 17). The "classic formulation" according to Langdon Gilkey is " . . . the word or symbol "God" has generally referred to one, supreme, or holy being, the unity of ultimate reality and ultimate goodness. So conceived, God is believed to have created the entire universe, to rule over it, and to intend to bring it to its fulfillment or realization, to "save" it." (p. 18). Sallie McFague has defined a model as "a metaphor that has gained sufficient stability and scope so as to present a pattern for relatively comprehensive and coherent explanation" (p. 34). She further contends that God the father is an example of such a model. In her argument, the author says "If God is seen as father, human beings become children, sin can be understood as rebellious behavior, and redemption can be thought of as a restoration to the status of favored offspring" (p. 34).

> The author wrote *Models of God* in an effort to have people look at the possibilities of new models of God that would be more in step with the needs of today's world.

Dynamic View

Sally McFague calls for a *de*construction of traditional imagery and suggests that theology should *re*mythologize the relationship between God and the world to meet the needs of today. She "experiments with new models such as God as mother, lover, and friend of the world, and with the image of the world as God's body" (p. xi). She continues by saying:

> If, to portray the Christian faith in the broadest strokes, it affirms the underlying direction of the universe to be on the side of life and its fulfillment—if, in other words, faith in God of the Judeo-Christian tradition is faith in the ultimate trustworthiness of things—then how, in our time and in metaphors and concepts appropriate to our time, can that faith be expressed with persuasive power?" (p. 29)

I believe that this can be best answered with her metaphor "God as friend." As McFague states: "the right name for those involved in this ongoing, sustaining, trustworthy, committed work for the world is neither parents nor lovers but friends (p. 165). As we perceive the complex meaning of friendship, we find that friendship represents a credible, appropriate model of God in keeping with the needs of today. Friendship is a free, bonding, reciprocal relationship that can unite across the typical boundaries of human beings and other forms of being and form an association committed to work for the world.

Relative View

   A. Classify your subject:

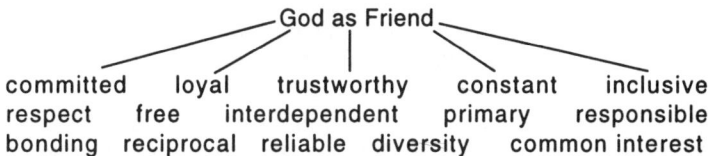

God as Friend

committed	loyal	trustworthy	constant	inclusive
respect	free	interdependent	primary	responsible
bonding	reciprocal	reliable	diversity	common interest

   B. Compare and contrast topic to other similar and dissimilar subjects.

God as Friend

Friends: My friends and I have common interests, respect, and are reliable. We are diverse, interdependent and yet free. My friends are also loyal, constant, and reciprocal.

Enemies: Unreliable, unpredictable. No respect. Most of the time not free—under an obligation—family or association.

Common interest and bonding absent.

Associates: Diverse with common interests. Bonding somewhat. Reciprocal is not like friends. Among all people—class structures different. This is not a relationship that is free. Commitment, yes. Trustworthy is questionable. Respect is forced, not free.

Family: Bonding, constant, and interdependent. With some there are common interests, reliability, respect. Our own family is inclusive, primary, interdependent, loyal, committed, and reciprocal.

Nature: My relationship with nature is common interest, reciprocal, and interdependent. I have a great deal of respect for the world and believe in underlining theme of models of God. It should be a primary issue to us all.

Animals: Relationships with animals are very special. Animals are trustworthy, loyal, reciprocal, and almost always committed to your enjoyment. Humans and animals have a unique bonding.

Industry: This relationship is definitely on shaky ground. I feel industry/business today (and maybe always) puts the interests of the world, society, and other beings in jeopardy by its self-serving commitments.

C. Analogy: My subject is like a *garment without thread.*

If the world can be seen as God's body then there is public call to protect it. The garment is the necessary clothing in which to protect God's body. I feel that God as a friend is an appropriate model (imagery) to promote this concept. It is so important it can be compared to the threads in a garment—without it, it would simply fall apart.

Doris has several more pages of specific quotes that are not included here. The exploration and the additional pages of relevant quotes form a rich base from which she can compose a draft. Overall, Doris has successfully captured her own ideas and explored her question.

Focus

After the rich exploration, students were asked to incubate, meaning that time away from their conscious efforts would let the unconscious synthesize the great amount of information they had gathered.

After at least one night off, students were asked to return to their original question and answer it in one sentence. The answer, or focus, becomes the thesis of the paper. This book was difficult for students. They formed a focus but allowed the first draft to solidify their ideas. Doris' focus is that McFague's metaphor of God as friend is credible and important, yet the other metaphors do not work as well.

Drafting

Students were assigned three versions of this essay. The first a free form version without concern for audience or mechanical correctness; the second a version concerned with strong development and organization; and the third a polished essay. These versions allow students to further trace out their thoughts and adapt them to the college reader. A conference with me was scheduled after the second version to refine the style. I gave comments on various aspects of the text after each of the first two versions.

Not all professors, even in English, assign multiple versions; I do so because I am not content with students' style on the second version. Doris' first and second versions are not included here because the differences among them are minor: At the end of this chapter another student's entire process is available in order to view changes in various drafts. What is important here is the comparison between Doris' beginning assignments and the final product. In the following third version, readers can see how parts of the exploration, as well as expansions of it, really develop the text. Unless these beginning wonderings are compared with the final versions (or interim versions), professors will never know whether students are learning. Furthermore, what is insightful to them might be overly familiar to the professor; the professor will not know whether students' work is powerful and important to them unless he or she knows how they began thinking about the assignment.

Doris' Third Version

In Doris' third version I am pleased with her use of the text, her arguments with it, and her own voice in her interpretation. The following is the third version:

> Theologians from the beginning of time have revised religion to adjust to the needs of their particular age. It is to this end that Sallie McFague wrote the thought provoking book,

Models of God. In an effort to *r*emythologize, McFague attempts to *de*mythologize the traditional imperialistic imagery for God and offers to her readers innovative alternatives. She feels that a new sensibility is needed to address the concerns of an ecological and nuclear age. "The single most important recognition for continuation, not to mention fulfillment, of life in our threatened nuclear world is the awareness that `we are not our own,' that we owe our existence to the life that came before us, and must pass life along to those who will come after" (p. 95).

Her experiment in remythologizing the gospel begins with an analogy—image—of the world as God's body. She feels that this relationship is appropriate for our time and conveys an "ethic of care" necessary for the survival of the world and all beings which inhabit it. Arguing the ineffectiveness of traditional outmoded perceptions of God ("God as king, ruler, lord, master, and governor") (p. 19), she boldly calls us to adopt new models of God that would represent mutuality, independence, caring, and responsiveness—characteristics in keeping with the concerns of today. Of the three metaphors suggested: God as mother, lover, and friend, I feel God as friend is the most credible and appropriate.

Although there appears to be no conclusive definition for the word friend, the general agreement is that friendship is something special. It is a relationship that "alone exists outside the bounds of duty, function, or office" (p. 159), rendering it the most free of all human relationships. Friendship is a reciprocal arrangement characterized by bonding, affection, respect and trust. People who are friends are united in common visions and are committed and loyal to each other. What better positive attributes to associate with God and the salvation of the world? Because we are free to be friends with any other, God as friend gives us a model in which human beings and other beings can live together interdependently without boundaries. This model says we are responsible and we can be counted on. "If God is the friend of the world, the one committed to it, who can be trusted never to betray it, who not only likes the world but has a vision for its well-being, then we as the special part of the body—the *imago dei*—are invited as friends of the Friend of the world to join in that vision and work for its fulfillment" (p. 165).

If one is to agree with Sallie McFague's argument that "theologians ought not merely interpret biblical and traditional metaphors and models but ought to remythologize, to search in contemporary life and its sensibility for images more appropriate to the expression of Christian faith in our time" (p.33), then God as Friend should be given serious consideration. Of all the models given, it is the most believable. For, if God the Father is inappropriate because human beings are seen as children, why isn't the same true for God as Mother? To address the needs of the new sensibility, that is, to recognize human responsibility in a nuclear age, the model of God as either parent must be dispelled.

And what of God as lover? Sallie McFague claims that "A heuristic theology plays with ideas in order to find out, searches for likely accounts rather than definitions. The object of this kind of theology is to suggest metaphors that create a shock of recogition" (p. 63). God as lover certainly possesses the shock value of a metaphor, but does it supply the necessary shock of recognition? I think not. Perhaps, it is too big an imaginative leap to follow. I find that the relationship of lovers is too *unstable* to have any value in our unprecedented nuclear age. In our society, lovers can mean anything from casual sex to long term commitments, extramarital affairs, gay relationships, or something created on TV. If each of us see "lover" in a different context, how can it be a valid, recognizable metaphor? The metaphor God as lover is rendered impotent when its meaning is fraught with so many different values. We do not need more uncertainty in our time. What is needed in our time is a strong relationship that we can all relate to: God as Friend.

The metaphor of friend is a basic, positive image that is easily recognizable. Whether we are young or old, friendship is a relationship that has significance to us. It encompasses a broad spectrum of possibilities. Parents, siblings, associates, animals, and even nature, can be our friends. What a perfect example to promote the interdependence concept, "the recognition that mature perception and activity in our world demands interrelating not only with other human beings but also with other forms of being, both nonhuman and divine" (p. 165). And, perhaps most importantly, the model of friend exhibits the necessary responsibility that seems to be so sorely lacking in our time. Friends stand at your side— ready and willing to lend a hand—committed. As Sallie McFague states, "The right name for those involved in this ongoing, sustaining, trustworthy committed work for the world is neither parents nor lovers but friends" (p. 165).

This was a challenging book for first-year students and yet with enough planning, drafting, peer reviews, and conferences, the students made great progress in their thinking and writing.

CONCLUSION

Professors may not want insight in writing all the time; mastery of the subject matter may be the outstanding goal in some classes rather than insight. When insight is the goal, however, long-range planning is necessary to ensure success. Planning exercises, multiple versions, and peer conferences—when they are steered by a pedagogy that considers writing a creative process that can lead to insight—help students considerably. Also necessary is the professor's own communication about how important she or he feels students' questions, ideas, and full-personed responses are. The insights of persons not represented in the classroom are important to include so that insights may not become blindnesses, as de Man (1983) said.

Berlin (1984), in an essay on writing instruction during this century, said that "the work of French poststructuralist language theory, of American neo-pragmatist philosophy, and of epistemic rhetorical theory has argued that language is at the center of the formation of consciousness" (p. 220). Insight through writing testifies as well to the power of language to uncover or recover deeply owned values. The benefits of insight for students—the peace, action, extended use, and personal ownership—may never be seen by professors, but may be experienced for years spurring further study as well.

What about the student who does not reach insight—does he or she benefit as well? Consider Matt, an endearing basketball player who consistently produced "D" quality second versions. After enough planning, drafting, peer reviews, and conferences, Matt wrote the following about McFague's book in his third version: "I was thoroughly disoriented and I did not like it at all. This made me feel vulnerable." Matt did not reach an insight in his third draft, but he did start asking important academic and personal questions rather than (as in past drafts) clinging to his original position without showing any understanding. Language, as Berlin stated, was helping him with the formation of consciousness. His greatest argument with McFague is in her refusal to use Scripture as the basis of her theology: Matt agrees that the metaphor for God as friend is solvent because he has deep friendships and values God as a friend, but he cannot figure out why she needs to rely on metaphorical theology. The following are the last two paragraphs of his essay in which he unearths his real questions:

Her proposal made me reevaluate my friendships and really think what they are and have been all about. Her attempt at disorientation/reorientation has left me in the latter part of this cycle. I am still trying to figure out how her views might enhance my own convictions. What she has done, is given me a greater appreciation for one of the institutions that I value the most, friendship. God is still one of my best friends. This is something that I have known all of my life and nothing will change this no matter what anyone says.

In conclusion, I still feel that people can imagine God in any form they wish. Here I agree with the attempts of the author to make God a little closer and more personal. God as a friend is an extraordinary model for people who value their friends. The only real problems that I have with the author and her proposals are the *real* underlying reasons: Why can she not make a proposal without ripping apart the very fabric of our religious experience? Why can she not make a proposal that will help *everyone* understand God a little better? By being more open about her initial motives for writing, she could only hope to receive more support and following. Ultimately, I still believe God is the *best* friend that anyone has and as Bonhoeffer is quoted in the book, friendship is the "rarest and most priceless treasure of all" (159).

Matt agrees with McFague but not on the same grounds. For a student like Matt to question is still a reasonable and important goal for his professor to reach. Someday he will most likely answer his questions and this course has helped him to do so with his full person.

A SECOND EXAMPLE

Another full example of a first-year student's work follows. Troy was enrolled in a first-year composition course, Writers Seminar, which could have been subtitled "The Quality of Men's Lives" because the class read and wrote about four books on masculinity. This essay concerns a book by Mark Gerzon (1982) titled *A Choice of Heroes*. Students were to ask a question concerning this or another book they read; from this question they were to plan, draft, revise, and edit three versions of their essay. They were also required to meet in peer groups and with their instructor. Included is all the work Troy completed over a 3-week period.

Troy's Planning, Draftings, and Essay

Planning

Starting Point

Question: Do sports repress men's feminine side? (Note: this question was preceded by previous questions, but Troy wasn't satisfied with any of them.)

Exploratory Guide
Static View

"All boys love baseball. If they don't they're not real boys (p. 195—Zane Grey)." It is generally accepted, if not through Gerzon, then life, that the realm of sports is deeply seated in the minds of men. Sports builds character. Young boys didn't have time to do anything but athletics. As Gerzon puts it, "I was too busy mastering skills, competing, and proving myself, I am grateful for the opportunity to build what coaches through the years invariably called a `good self-image' (156—Gerzon)." The strive for success has always been rooted in our psyche. As a child I remember my father pitching balls to me. Though there was never outside pressure to perform, the drive was inner. Picture a three year old striking on a pitch and laughing, exclaiming "I mit!" There was support from my father to hit the ball. Inside I know there was something more. I wanted, no I needed to hit that ball to prove—at least to myself—that I could hit it. It was the drive, the personal competition that enabled me to "mit" the ball repeatedly. Had I been disgruntled instead of determined, I would have thrown the bat away and cried to mommy. Even at the young age of three, I was taught to be a winner, "moments of glory were possible on [the] field" (p. 155-Gerzon). I was not to succumb to the weaker parts of my mind. I was not to show "negative" emotions during the game. I was a big boy. Big boys don't cry. Only girls cry. "The boys on the ice with their skates, there is a stone on the ice. One boy did not see it, and has had a fall. But he is a brave boy and will not cry" (p. 155-McGuffey's Primer). The truly emotional side of us has been stripped away by our peers calling after the cryer—"Go ahead, run to mother, you wus. We don't want to play with girls." Where did this come from.

Dynamic View

I grew up playing baseball, soccer, basketball, and tennis.

Tennis was last on the list of priorities to participate in because it wasn't a contact sport—or so we thought. Any non-contact sport, of course, is feminine by nature and shouldn't be played by boys. Tennis is now my favorite sport. I gave up baseball because it *wasn't physical enough*. I stuck with soccer from the age of seven until the end of 8th grade when an injury forced me out. What I loved about soccer was the brutality that could be inflicted. It sounds sick, but I was goalie; I either had to be crazy or I would get hurt. I ultimately did get hurt, but it was while running—noncontact—feminine. With the exception of football, basketball I feel involves the most contact. Yet it is not a contact sport. I stopped playing basketball at the end of last season because I was tired of it, burnt out. What I liked most about it was that I could bang bodies and be nasty to people. It was an escape for my emotions. I am generally pretty docile; all of the pent up animosities of life were released through basketball. But now as I mentioned earlier, it is tennis now. I still hear it referred to as a "pussy sport, played by women," but I don't care anymore. I just tell the person to call Boris Becker or Stephan Edberg a pussy to his face and his checking account. I think insecurity is a big factor as to why people degrade others. The only people to comment on my playing tennis are the ones that have limited athletic ability. I don't feel bad or embarrassed because I play, and I should. I have stopped "neglecting, or actively suppressing other sides of my personality because they were not part of this arbitrary sexual accounting" (p. 156-Gerzon). Tennis is the most personal competitiveness I can achieve at this point in my life. "Masculinity equals competitiveness" (p. 161-Gerzon). If I play tennis, I am masculine. If that is the case, tennis is not a feminine sport.

I have just avoided my own femininity—It wasn't intentional—why should I prove to others that tennis isn't a "fag" sport?

Relative View

A. Classify your subject.

competition—winner—man—glory—heroes—good self-image don't cry—non-contact—pussy—fag—men compete—girls on bleachers—masculinity=competitiveness—we don't play with girls

B. Compare and contrast your subject to other subjects.

military—making the most out of the male body—completely ripping away all femininity

Arnold S.—the complete image of a man—try calling him a girl

Hans & Frans—Saturday Night Live version of Arnold's calling—"Get away from us you girly-man before we break your puny legs with our fingers."

Gambling—a night out with the boys. Time to slam a few beers and act as tough as possible while tell crude jokes about women

Risk taking—sky divers and bungi jumpers—men out to prove themselves men by risking death

Richard Simmons—the most feminine person I know

gymnastics—traditionally a women's sport considered a "queer" if done by a man

housekeeping—women's work, her place is in the home

Dance—the feminine art—like gymnastics—man is considered "queer"

The arts—women's showcase of expression—the only reason a man would get into the arts would be that he isn't athletic therefore he isn't masculine

C. Create an analogy for your subject.

Sports contribute to taking the femininity out of a man are like a swing. They take a lot of energy to learn the "rules" (can't cry, etc), but once you have the rules down, it takes little energy to keep going. The game becomes automatic, too much fun to stop. Once you've learned to play, it is impossible to forget. You can get into many of these activities simply by jumping off. But you always return to the starting point, learning the rules of the new game. Eventually you learn that nothing has changed—"we don't play with girls."

First Version

[Assignment: Sit down and write—no concern for anything except answering your question for yourself on paper—no concern for grammar, spelling, punctuation. Just ideas, and have fun. Write for yourself.]

His voice was enough to intimidate me, as well as my teammates. A heavily accented English baritone that on many occasions bellowed for miles. Soccer was in his blood, and he did all in his power, short of physical violence, to open our vessels to his passion. He sculpted his players into mechanical specimens simply through the fear of his wrath. Mistakes were not tolerated, his discipline was exceptionally brutal. Victory was everything. A defeat was a one-way ticket straight into his hell.

Many on the team, including myself, hated this man for the self-degradation he put us through. He made us men, though, at least most of the time. I remember specifically his words when we did not perform perfectly:

"You are playing like a bunch of girls out there, a bunch of pansy-assed girls! If you could only see the way you women are playing out there, its disgraceful. My two year old is more of a man than any of you. And you, Funk, what the hell are you doing in this game? You are supposed to sacrifice your body for the sake of the team. Forget about the pain and throw yourself in front of the ball. This is soccer for Christ sake, not a fucking ballet. Let's go girls, they aren't going to give you the game, you have to rip the victory straight from their balls. Put your whole heart into the effort and win this damn game. We will win this game or you girls won't have enough time this week to call your mother's name in your sleep. Is this all clear? It better be."

I was twelve years old at the time and the starting goalie for my town traveling soccer team. At this point in the game we were winning one-nothing. The final score of the game was seven-nothing.

Throughout my six years with this man, I saw many of my friends quit the team, reduced to tears from my coach's mental batterings. It was taboo to cry in front of this man. He would not tolerate it. Eventually, after being hardened, it was taboo to cry in front of anyone for any reason. We could not afford to be weak in front of him. "We strived to show [him] that we were real men, which means that anything vaguely feminine about us had been discarded like outgrown clothes." He made us pawns, machines to do his killing. He successfully stripped us of our feminine weaknesses.

Winning is the name of the game. Sides are picked on the playground for the sole purpose of winning the event. Whether a boy is picked or not depends on his ability to make an impact toward the team's success. Friends aren't pitted against each other in fun and games, "it is boy against boy competition" from the start.

From an early age, boys are taught the difference between

winning and losing in a very simple manner. The winner is the one jumping around and goofing off on the way home, while the loser slumbers off alone, dragging his feet, eyes staring into nothingness seeking internal solace. Parents did more to instill victory as the main aspect of athletics whether they were conscious of it or not. Picture the scene. A grass stained boy with a baseball glove tucked under his arm walks through the front door. His closing of the door is greeted from the T.V. room couch, where his father rests watching a football game, with, "Hey champ, did you win." If he won the game, he rushed into the T.V. room and tells his dad all about the game. If however, he loses, he walks to the stairs and quietly mumbles, "No." His dad replies, "Tough luck kid, maybe next time." Nothing else is mentioned after this exchange. The victory is talked about for days. With each new entrance through that front door, the boy's mind is getting reinforced into thinking that victory is the only reason for competition; fun comes with winning.

Competing involves both winning and losing. Boys are taught that victory is intrinsically bound to success. What they are never taught about, is the second half of competition; defeat. Sure, they are taught how to handle defeat, "never show your disappointment until you are off the field; never take anything away from your opponents victory; be gracious in defeat, because there is always a next time," but they are never taught how to accept it.

The word defeat then is an excuse to go out and compete again. There always is a next time. Rivalries are formed, pitting boy against boy until a dominance is established through repetitive beatings. Everything about sports ultimately comes down to who is better.

Always on a team there is one performer who stands out among his peers in presence and ability. This player is recognized and celebrated for his achievements in front of his teammates. This creates a healthy jealousy driving the players to reach the same celebrated status. Improvement is tracked and charted, also criticized. If a desired level of improvement is not reached, the player will be benched, ridiculed, and eventually fired from the team; all in an attempt to aid the team in avoiding humiliation in defeat. It is a vicious cycle aimed at creating the perfect athlete and the perfect team. Flawlessness is difficult to achieve. That is why only the smartest, strongest, and most determined can ever obtain it. Perfection can be reached only by 100% man. "Girls remain on the bleachers," as mere supporters to their men.

Society created sports to make boys men. "Masculinity equals competitiveness; men compete." For young boys, the sporting arena was the battlefield where competitiveness was personified. No other place could a boy become a man in one afternoon. Society as a whole has exploited this. Town leagues are established to make boys into men. All of the virtues of masculinity are lived by on the field. The men of society are used as role models, teachers, and coaches. They are the ones that shape our youth. It was society that appointed a member of the Wales National Soccer Team to be my coach. They had a direct hand in the feeding of the masculine qualities and the regurgitation of the feminine. Millions like me have lost half of their humanness in the quest for victory. It is society that has screamed for victory and booed defeat. Society has taught us to measure ourselves, "against a standard of masculinity that omitted many of the most vital qualities a man can possess."

Instructor's Response to First Version

Troy

Excellent first draft. I'm really appalled at how boys are coached. Can't believe this happened when you were only 12! One note: do you see how, with the word "self-degradation" you buy into the notion that being called or equated female is degrading?
Focus: Sports make boys repress thier feminine sides.
    Clear.
Development: 1. *excellent* language quote from coach. It
            makes paper.
          2. need another intro—you know that
          3. I'd like you to analyze the coach's language
            just a bit—you go back to the usual stuff
            about winning afterward rather that dis-
            cussing how sports condition men to
            repress their feminine side by attacking it.
            Threat of homosexuality is there too. Use
            Gerzon.

Organization: This is pretty good. I'll work with your paragraphs a bit on the second draft.

Audience Guide

[Assignment: Consider who your audience is, how much he or she knows about your topic, how strongly opinions are held. Note: the following exercise does not relate to Troy's essay; it pertains to a professor in another course.]

My audience is a man in his 40's with a PhD who is primarily concerned with Latin American governments. The problem with writing for this man is that he doesn't value differing opinions even when they can be backed up and substantiated by quotes from a source book. He really values thinking, especially detailed analysis. He wants his students to give a lot of effort. If he sees they aren't trying, he asks them really specific questions to nail them to the wall. He appears to be an expert on everything and has an opinion on everything. His opinion is always right. The only way to please this man is to agree with his opinion. I can't do that all the time so I must be extremely creative in my persuasive attempts of conveying my opinion. When he likes something a lot he always laughs, kind of a low gutteral chuckle.

Organizational Plan

[Assignment: Answer the question who is suffering in order to put social significance into your introduction; then present the order in which you will develop your focus.]

Who is suffering? I think man is because he is repressing his natural tendency of feminism* through the pursuit of excellence in sports. Society is allowing this to continue by appointing coaches that epitomize the macho-never-say-die attitude.

I. choose to answer my question in three parts:

I. establish how sports make men robots for victory

II. how coaches help to shape this

III. how society makes sports continuously masculine, never curbing their thinking to the more feminine side of life. I have to state an opinion for each of these three issues and then find quotes or use past experiences to back up my opinion.

I. using quotes about child development I showed that kids (male) are brought up to know only victory and not defeat. I want to show that by repressing defeat, boys are already on their way to repressing feminism.

II. I used a personal experience to show how powerful the forces repressing feminism really are. By using a more personal example I instill in the reader and myself, that I have a slanted view of this topic. I was taught to repress feminism. I am angry at this, that is why this paper slams sports.

---

*He probably means to be feminine but we are faithful to his text.

III. I need to work on this part; I want to show that society has a hand in this issue. I'm not sure how to relate it because I can't find any good quotes or a personal experience to accurately fit. I suppose I could make one up to fit, but I want to keep this as real as possible.

Shifting Voices Exercise

[Assignment: Briefly tell four different audiences your topic. Listen to yourself shift voices.]

1. Dear Mom:
   I'm writing this paper on how sports repress the feminine side of men. I don't know how I'm gonna do it, but it will be interesting.
2. Dear Smitty [high school English teacher]:
   I'm writing a paper on how sports repress the feminine side of men. Do you think they do?
3. Dear Senator:
   I've got a problem. I have to write a paper on how sports repress the feminine side of men. You were an athlete, what is your opinion on this issue?
4. Dear Barf [best friend]:
   I'm writing a paper on how sports repress the feminine side of men. Wow, just had a thought—they also increase the masculinity of women. Sounds like good stuff huh. How's Bowdoin?

Second Version

[Assignment: Draft a paper, not necessarily anything like the first paper, in which you concentrate on focus, development, and organization.]

Do sports contribute to man's repression of his feminine side? There is one way that I must attack this question. It is broken up into three parts. I must first establish the ways in which sporting rules centralize man's thinking, thus creating a robot incapable of defeat, the first sign of weakness. Next I have to establish the general attitudes of athletes that have been shaped into machines by men of the system, namely, the coaches that have stripped away the capacity for expression in their machines. Finally I must focus on how society interprets sporting events; whether sports are a tool for making a man a whole man or only a piece of the real thing.

When you get right down to it, winning is the name of the game. When sides are chosen, "Those chosen first are best; those chosen last are worst. And the one who sits out is the worst of all." Friends don't play against friends, "It is boy against boy competition." The only criteria for choosing teams is "whether having him on the team makes winning more likely."

Because defeat is part of any sport, boys are taught how to handle it. Be gracious in defeat, never let the other guy know how disappointed you are with losing, that only makes his victory all the sweeter. There is always a next time. And there always is. Rivalries are formed, pitting boy against boy until a dominance is established through repetitive beatings. Victory is central. Everything about sports ultimately comes down to who is better. The better man is always the one that wins. Records are kept to track team and individual dominance. Even on a team there is a star, one who stands out among his peers in presence and ability. The best on the team is rewarded with a medal or a trophy, even a day off from practice. Individual's progress is also tracked and compared to earlier stats to encourage a player to perform better. Through peer pressure, a competitor will improve through fear of ridicule. If there is no improvement, he will be forced off the team by his peers in attempt to replace him with someone better. It is a vicious cycle all aimed at creating the perfect athlete and the perfect team. A robotic team that executes with precision and perfection is desired at all times. The only standard for measuring a team's perfection is by matching one team against another in one on one competition. A team going undefeated is considered perfect for that season. Flawlessness is difficult to achieve. That is why only the smartest, the strongest, and the most determined can ever obtain it. Perfection can only be reached by 100% man. "Girls remain on the bleachers" as mere supporters to their men.

Once perfection, or at least near perfection has been reached, the athlete takes his knowledge and passes it along to someone lacking the elitest-type standard of perfection. This is called coaching. Parents and other minor adult figures can attempt to teach their children how to play, but that is far different than coaching. Parents pass on limited knowledge and sometimes contradictory knowledge to their children. Fun seems to be the intention of such teachers. They are only introducing the child to the sport, providing the child with a false sense of knowledge, thus creating a false sense of security when facing peers on the battle ground. Only a true coach can convey the killer win-all attitude needed for success.

One man provided me with this attitude. He was my coach for six years for a traveling soccer team in my town. He played for the National Team of Wales before he moved to the United States. His voice alone was enough to intimidate me as well as my teammates. A heavily English accented baritone that could bellow for miles. Soccer was in his blood, and he did all in his power short of physical violence to open our vessels to his passion. He made my teammates and I into perfect physical specimens simply through fear of his punishments. Mistakes were not tolerated, his discipline was exceptionally brutal. All his conditioning and scare tactics shaped *his* team into the perfect battalion, stamping out opposition of all sizes. Victory was everything. A defeat was a ticket straight into his hell.

Many on the team, including myself, hated this man for the self-degradation he put us through. He made us men though, at least most of the time. I remember specifically his words when we did not perform perfectly. "You are playing like a bunch of girls out there, a bunch of pansy-assed girls. If you could only see the way you women are playing out there. My two-year old is more of a man than any of you. And you Funk, what the hell are you doing in the game? You are supposed to sacrifice your body for the sake of the team. Forget about the pain and throw yourself in front of the ball. This is soccer for Christ's sake, not a fucking ballet. Let's go girls, they aren't going to give the game to you, you have to rip the victory from their balls. Put your whole heart into the effort and win this damn game. We will win this game or you girls won't have enough time this week to say your boyfriend's name in your sleep." I was twelve years old at the time and the starting goalie. We won the game seven-nothing.

Throughout my six years with this man, I saw many of my friends quit the team, reduced to tears from my coach's mental and emotional batterings. It was taboo to cry in front of this man. He would not tolerate it. Eventually, after being hardened, it was taboo to cry in front of anyone for any reason. We could not afford to be weak anymore. "We strived to show [him] that we were real men, which means that anything vaguely feminine about us had been discarded like outgrown clothes." He made us pawns, machines to do his killing. He successfully stripped us of our feminine weaknesses.

Society holds a great part in the shaping of young boys. Men are used as role models, as heroes for the youth of today. It is the adult world that has a hand in molding the younger generation. The men, teachers and coaches alike, instruct the boys in the same way they were taught in their childhood. Winning is still the focal point, not fun. It is still "the thrill of victory and the agony of defeat." The baseball field was the perfect location society could set aside to teach boys how to become men. "Shaped like the hardest of all precious stones, the diamond was a gymnasium of American Virtues. The true athlete could rise to heroism. Moments of glory were possible on those dusty fields."

Society created sports to make boys men. "Masculinity equals competitiveness; men compete." For young boys, the sporting arena was the battlefield where competitiveness was personified. No other place could a child become a man in one afternoon. Society as a whole exploited this. Town leagues are designed to teach boys about becoming men. All of the virtues of masculinity are lived by on the field. If the rules aren't followed the game is void.

Men were made on the ball fields, at least shells of men. Once the glory of victory was over and the real world smashed many young men in the face, sports were an irrelevant piece of the past that slanted males' interpretation of themselves. The only redeeming quality sports can hold in the real world is that of the business world. The never say die, fight until the end qualities are used in everyday business practices. But look at the business men, the lawyers and congressmen. Tattered shells of human souls with little remorse for their actions. They will go the whole nine yards for the win. Compassion and gentleness were lost in the hardening of our youths because of sports. Femininity has been stripped away, fumbled in the long drive for completeness. Only a portion of the child remains in the man. Half of his humanness lost in the quest for victory. All along society has aided this quest. Until this is realized by more people, a complete *human* man will not be formed. Athletics strip away men's feminine side in order to achieve victory. "We learned to measure other boys, and ourselves, against a standard of masculinity that omitted many of the most vital qualities a man can possess."

Third Version

[Assignment: After a conference with the instructor for style, correct and polish your prose and fix any organizational or development problems. Note: in conference I asked Troy why he wrecked the second draft with such heavy organization at the onset and ignored my advice about analyzing the coach's language. We spent the conference discussing these things.]

Do sports contribute to men's repression of their feminine side? If this is the case, the majority of men in today's society have been denied an important faculty of manhood. Sociologist Mark Gerzon strikes this chord when saying "we are divided against ourselves. As long as this division remains, the certainty of manhood will elude us" (p. 167).

Let us first consider the ways in which sporting rules centralize men's thinking, thus creating robots incapable of defeat, the first sign of weakness. Next, see how coaches have stripped away the capacity for expression in their machines. And finally we will focus on how society interprets sporting events; whether sports are a tool for making a man a whole man or only a piece of the real thing.

When you get down to it, winning is the name of the game. Gerzon, in his book, puts it best in his interpretation of the ritual choosing of teams: "Sides are chosen by two boys, who take turns picking their teammates. Those chosen first are best; those chosen last are worst. And the one who sits out is the worst of all. [Friends don't play against friends,] it is boy-against-boy competition. [The only criteria for choosing a team is] whether having him on the team makes winning more likely" (p. 160). Gerzon makes no mention of the involvement of girls in the realm of choosing sides. By this fact, he is backing up his theory about societal trends rendering sporting experiences antithetical to femininity.

From an early age, one is taught the difference between winning and losing. Little kids could see the winners jumping around on each other while the losers slumbered off alone, hanging their heads, seeking internal solace. The first word out of his father's mouth when his son comes through the door is undoubtedly, "did you win?" Not, "how did you play," or "did you have fun at the game today?" The boy is taught that victory is the only reason for competition; fun comes with winning.

Because defeat is part of any sport, boys are taught how to handle it. I learned to handle defeat in the following way. Be gracious in defeat, never let the other guy know how disappointed you are with losing, that only makes his victory all the sweeter. There is always a next time. And there always is. Rivalries are formed, pitting boy against boy until a dominance is established through repetitive beatings. Victory is central. Everything about sports ultimately comes down to who is better. The better man is the one that wins.

To break down the competitive infrastructure of team dominance further is the concept of player recognition. On every team there is a star performer, one who stands out among his fellow teammates. The star is highly touted by society as the essence of what the rest of the team should represent. There is a public pressure for the lower caliber teammates to raise their level of ability so it matches that of the star. This public ridicule, as a sociologist would say, is a call to establish a norm. A deviant of this norm is not tolerated. The cry for the highest level of ability can only be met by the smartest, strongest, and most determined of individuals. Society calls on men to have all these masculine characteristics. The feminine side of men must be repressed in order to conform to society's established norm. An effort to avoid this repression is exactly that which is ridiculed.

Once society's call has been answered, the athlete takes his knowledge and passes it along to someone lacking the elitest-type standard of perfection. This is called coaching. Parents can attempt to teach their children how to play, but that is far different than coaching. Parents pass on limited, general, and sometimes contradictory knowledge to their children. Fun seems to be the intention of such teachers. They are only introducing the child to the sport, providing him with a false sense of knowledge, thus creating a false sense of security when facing peers on the battle ground. Only a true coach can convey the killer win-all attitude needed for success. A sociologist, such as Gerzon, would note that it is not enough to be taught by parents, a specialist is truly necessary for competitive survival.

One man provided me with this attitude. He was my coach for 6 years for a traveling soccer team in my town. He played for the National Team of Wales before he moved to the United States. His voice alone was enough to intimidate me as well as my teammates. A heavily English accented baritone that could bellow for miles. Soccer was in his blood, and he did all in his power short of physical violence to open our vessels to his passion. He made my teammates and I into perfect physical specimens simply through fear of his punishments. Mistakes were not tolerated, his discipline was exceptionally brutal. All his conditioning and scare tactics shaped *his* team into the perfect battalion, stamping out opposition of all sizes. Victory was everything. A defeat was a ticket straight into his hell.

Many on the team, including myself, hated this man for the self-degradation he put us through. He made us men though, at least most of the time. I remember specifically his words when we did not perform perfectly:

You are playing like a bunch of girls out there, a bunch of pansy-assed girls. If you could only see the way you women are playing out there. My two-year old is more of a man than any of you. And you Funk, what the hell are you doing in the game? You are supposed to sacrifice your body for the sake of the team. Forget about the pain and throw yourself in front of the ball. This is soccer for Christ's sake, not a fucking ballet. Let's go girls, they aren't going to give the game to you, you have to rip the victory from their balls. Put your whole heart into the effort and win this damn game. We will win this game or you girls won't have enough time this week to say your boyfriend's name in your sleep.

I was 12 years old at the time and the starting goalie. We won the game seven-nothing.

By attacking his players with the slandering of women and related feminine traits, my coach conditioned us to resent and throw away the femininity within ourselves. Stressing that any feminine aspect made us vulnerable to persecution, he made it a sin for us to even remotely equate ourselves with the opposite sex and to sympathize with homosexuals.

Throughout my six years with this man, I saw many of my friends quit the team, reduced to tears from my coach's mental and emotional batterings. It was taboo to cry in front of this man. He would not tolerate it. Eventually, after being hardened, it was taboo to cry in front of anyone for any reason. We could not afford to be weak anymore. Mark Gerzon, in his book, interprets the concept like this: "We strived to show [him] that we were real men, which means that anything vaguely feminine about us had been discarded like outgrown clothes" (p. 167). He made us pawns, machines to do his killing. He successfully stripped us of our feminine weaknesses.

Society holds a great part in the shaping of young boys. Men are used as role models, as heroes for the youth of today. It is the adult world that has a hand in molding the younger generation. The men, teachers and coaches alike, instruct the boys in the same way they were taught in their childhood. Winning is still the focal point, not fun. It is still "the thrill of victory and the agony of defeat." The baseball field was the perfect location society could set aside to teach boys how to become men. Mark Gerzon uses the following metaphor to instill this. "Shaped like the hardest of all precious stones, the diamond was a gymnasium of American Virtues. The true athlete could rise to heroism. Moments of glory were possible on those dusty fields" (p. 155).

Society created sports to make boys men. Gerzon says, "Masculinity equals competitiveness; men compete" (p. 161). For young boys, the sporting arena was the battlefield where competitiveness was personified. No other place could a child become a man in one afternoon. Society as a whole exploited this. Town leagues are designed to teach boys about becoming men. All of the virtues of masculinity are lived by on the field. If the rules aren't followed the game is void.

Men were made on the ball fields, at least shells of men. Once the glory of victory was over and the real world smashed many young men in the face, sports were an irrelevant piece of the past that slanted males' interpretation of themselves. The only redeeming quality sports can hold in the real world is that of the business world. The never-say-die, fight-until-the-end qualities are used in everyday business practices. But look at the business men, the lawyers and congressmen. Tattered shells of human souls with little remorse for their actions. They will go the whole nine yards for the win. Compassion and gentleness were lost in the hardening of our youths because of sports. Femininity has been stripped away, fumbled in the long drive for completeness. Only a portion of the child remains in the man. Half of his humanness lost in the quest for victory. All along society has aided this quest. Until this is realized by more people, a complete *human* man will not be formed. Athletics strip away men's feminine side in order to achieve victory. Sociologist Mark Gerzon agrees saying "we learned to measure other boys, and ourselves, against a standard of masculinity that omitted many of the most vital qualities a man can possess" (p. 156).

6

Insight, Mystery
and Art

Toward the end of his book-length study of insight, Lonergan
(1957/1978) admitted to a surprising but understandable
impasse. No stranger to writing on realms of the mysterious, he
realized that humans will always have more questions than
answers. Paradoxically, at a time when so much is known about
the worlds within, between, and about us, and from a variety of
perspectives, insight cannot resolve all of these manifold questions and dissonances. The answer, claimed Lonergan and several
other writers, is to enhance our knowledge of insight, of course,
but also to turn the problem over to another sphere of learning.
He wrote:

> adequate self-knowledge and explicit metaphysics may con-
> tract but cannot eliminate a 'known unknown,' and . . . they
> cannot issue into a control of human living without being
> transported into dynamic images which make sensible to
> human sensitivity what human intelligence reaches for or
> grasps. (p. 548)

The dynamic images he spoke of are myth and images that he proposed can yield insight when other efforts fail. This chapter
examines Lonergan's claim and presents some techniques taken
from the work of art theorist Margaret Miles (1985) on using
art to arrive at insight.

EXAMPLE

An example of what Lonergan described can be found in the experience of Bender in her book *Plain and Simple* (1989) in which
she described the effect of Amish quilts. Another is the Fire Watch
epilogue in *The Sign of Jonas* (1953) by Merton in which he too
integrated profound questions with his immediate surroundings of
the old monastery and the knobs of Kentucky. Both writers articulated serious, prolonged dissonances surrounding their lives, and
both, through a combination of using image and writing, came to
great insight.

  The shock of recognition that the image has something to do
with one's state of mind is well illustrated in Bender's first look
at the quilts:

> Twenty years ago I walked into Latham's Men's Store in Sag
> Harbor, New York, and saw old quilts used as a background
> for men's tweeds. I had never seen quilts like that. Odd color
> combinations. Deep saturated solid colors: purple, mauve,
> green, brown, magenta, electric blue, red. Simple geometric
> forms: squares, diamonds, rectangles. A patina of use
> emanated from them. They spoke directly to me. They knew
> something. They went straight to my heart. . . . The quilts
> spoke to such a deep place inside me that I felt them reaching
> out, trying to tell me something, but my mind was thorough-
> ly confused. How could pared-down and daring go together?
> How could a quilt be calm and intense at the same time? Can
> an object do that? Can an object know something? (pp. 1-3)

There was no way in Bender's busy world of work, art, and family
obligations that any answers to her need for integration and
wholeness could be found. The interesting point on which Lonergan
would have us ponder is that the quilt itself—without having been
known or understood—drew Bender into a deep search that enabled
her to integrate her intellect, emotions, and values. He wrote that
a person's "advance in self-knowledge implies increasing consciousness and deliberateness and effectiveness in his choice and

use of dynamic images, of mottoes and slogans" (p. 548). Bender eventually used the theories behind the images to sculpt her life as she wished. She researched the Amish and even found a way to live with two families for weeks at a time.

Implicit in the two questions at the end of Bender's quote just given is the desire to integrate seemingly opposing qualities that she viewed Amish quilts embodying. Belenky et al. (1986), in *Women's Ways of Knowing*, wrote of this ability to be drawn by intuition as one of the ways women in particular (but perhaps more so how minorities) develop in individuation and responsibility. Their text considers subjective thought synonymous with self-definition and autonomy rather than with delusion. The most highly developed women in Belenky et al.'s book were those "constructivist" knowers who integrated their inner voices with knowledge gained from others, and who were able to "actively reflect on how their judgments, attitudes, and behavior coalesce into some internal experience of moral consistency" (p. 150).

Bender found, after manifold attempts at integrating various Amish principles into her daily life, an interesting balance in the form of nine insights (corresponding to the Nine Patch quilt pattern she first learned). The following is the last patch and a further reflection:

PATCH #9 CHOICE
Before I went to the Amish, I thought that the more choices I had, the luckier I'd be. But there is a big difference between having many choices and making a choice. Making a choice—declaring what is essential—creates a framework for a life that eliminates many choices but gives meaning to the things that remain. Satisfaction comes from giving up wishing I was somewhere else or doing something else. (p. 141)

The biggest surprise—and it came as a great revelation—was understanding that whatever happens, no matter how catastrophic or wonderful, it's just another patch. There are times when something special happens: a marriage, graduation, or the birth of a child. There's no denying it's a glorious patch. It might even be a *red* patch—the one that pulls the whole quilt together. But I couldn't stop repeating, "It's just another patch." (p. 142)

Lonergan believed the result of insight was responsibility, that once aware of whatever needed to be considered, people would assume responsibility for it. Bender well illustrated this principle in her realistic application of Amish principles.

INSIGHT FROM IMAGES

Dulles, Merton, and Miles provided some academic discussions on the experience of insight from images.

In a chapter on symbolic mediation, Dulles (1985) summarized a number of modern theologians' thoughts on how images yield insights and defined *symbol* as "a sign pregnant with a plenitude of meaning which is evoked rather than explicitly stated" (p. 132). He wrote that symbol "introduces us to realms of awareness not normally accessible to discursive thought" because the symbol opens what was previously unavailable to consideration. They can "generate an indefinite series of particular insights" because they put us "in touch with deeper aspects of reality" (p. 137). Merton (1955) more fully described the process:

> The soul that picks and pries at itself in the isolation of its own dull self-analysis arrives at a self-consciousness that is a torment and a disfigurement of our whole personality. But the spirit that finds itself above itself in the intensity and cleanness of its reaction to a work of art is "self-conscious" in a way that is productive as well as sublime. Such a one finds in himself totally new capacities for thought and vision and moral action. Without a moment of self-analysis he has discovered himself in discovering his capacity to respond to a value that lifts him above his normal level. His very response makes him better and different. He is conscious of a new life and new powers, and it is not strange that he should proceed to develop them. (pp. 34-35)

The "participatory knowledge" and "transforming effect" of art on the viewer that Merton described are also important claims of which Dulles wrote. They correspond to the writings on insight from various disciplines in that insight from images "involves the knower as a person" (p. 137). Dulles quoted Eliade saying that "'the symbol is thus able to reveal a perspective in which heterogeneous realities are susceptible of articulation into a whole' thus enabling human life to be integrated into the totality of being" (p. 138).

Nevertheless, the use of art for insight is not common. The average viewer is inundated with commercial images and ignorant of the conscious use of them. Miles (1985) wrote that this situation was not true of the viewer in history:

The historical viewer, on the other hand, expected images to present a world in which reality and values were organized in an absolute, harmonized, and permanent configuration. The historical viewer expected to contemplate the image and be formed by it; he or she did not expect to receive information from it or to evaluate it critically. (p. 128)

Images that are commercial, she said, "promote sexism, racism, and agism, creating by the endless repetition of these visual clichés 'marginal' people who can never realistically aspire to youth, wealth, the right skin color, or sexual preference to qualify for the satisfaction promised by the image" (p. 133). Commercial images are not ones of ontological significance that enable viewers to gain in distance and subjectivity and thereby contemplate meaning in their own lives. Thus, it is important to cultivate ways to consciously implement images in search of insight.

TECHNIQUES OF USING IMAGE FOR INSIGHT

Like Lonergan, Miles advocated a conscious choosing of images by which one wishes to be formed. The selection of these images is largely an intuitive venture that is solidified through reflection and analysis.

To select positive images, one must also discard destructive ones. The "Seven Sisters" (Redbook, McCalls and the like) are having financial problems most probably because the images they present of women are so destructive. The women, in their activities and concerns, are shown to be nothing less than frantic, overextended, and exhausted. Of central focus are women's fears, sexuality, and bonds to others rather than their independence, strength, resourcefulness, and even joy. To spot the effect of images, Miles advised changing the viewing conditions: Flipping quickly through a magazine, or spending a greater amount of time than usual loosen the image from its typically commercial setting wherein it sells a product or illustrates a concern. Focusing on the possible tensions between an image and the language of the advertisement can also be a source of information.

Once images have been isolated that the viewer intuits to be either destructive or positive, Miles advised asking questions. One tries to discern whether the image fortifies one's being: As Miles put it, "can I locate, in my daily fare of images, a supply of images that affirm me and help me to explore what it is to be a woman of my age in my culture? Or do media images tell me that I am the wrong sex, the wrong age, or the wrong color?" (p. 148). After much searching through images, Miles advised forming a portfolio of images by which one wishes to be formed: "Select and develop a repertoire of images, chosen because they attract and because from them one receives visual messages that help one to visualize—to envision—personal and social transformation and thus to focus the energy of attention and affection with more clarity" (pp. 148-149). She noted that the viewer might engage in searches for historical and modern images.

Images express or compensate, according to Miles. In forming one's portfolio of images, she noted that it may be of use to collect images that express what the viewer wishes to develop in expression along with images that compensate for what the viewer does not have the chance in daily life to develop. Bender, for instance, used the Amish quilts to compensate for the lack of unity, harmony, and stillness: More importantly, however, her continued presence in front of the image, or contemplation of the image and discovery of what ideas caused the quilt to be composed as it was, eventually ushered Bender into the insights that enabled her to implement what the image symbolized. The image became her insight—over time, through study, and through active engagement of the principles for which it stood. Such is the purpose of collecting images; after one has collected a set of them, Miles advised a continued presence for self-reflection in order to allow the insights to become manifest.

IMAGES FOR INSIGHT IN COLLEGE WRITING: A STUDENT ESSAY

The process of using images for insight as discussed by Miles is enhanced in higher education when various ways of interpreting images in cultures are proposed and students are encouraged to integrate them with their own experiences, values, and thoughts. The essay that follows was completed by a student enrolled in a 300-level economics seminar on Thorstein Veblen. Rather than approach Veblen's theory of the leisure class as independent and abstract, this student wove together her own questions and behavior with Veblen's interpretations and in so doing arrived at insight. Too often, however, such reflection and integration are not allowed in college classrooms. The following is Sarajane's essay:

The scene could be any suburban shopping mall. All over the country, no matter where I go, it's there. I cross the threshold and breathe deeply, the soft scent of potpourri caressing my nostrils. I tell myself that I'm only here to look, to immerse myself momentarily in a world of silks, satins, and lace. Of course, I know that I'm only fooling myself; it isn't long before my eyes glaze over and my brain swims lazily in the fog that fills my head. I'm in a consumer frenzy, overcome by the desire to purchase wildly expensive lingerie at Victoria's Secret.

The phenomenal success of Victoria's Secret, part of the Limited Corporation, surprised many people, but not me. Why would women pay grossly inflated prices for unnecessary and often highly uncomfortable garments that (one assumes) no one except she and her dearly beloved will see? More specifically, why would I, a poor college student, spend hundreds of dollars on items that ultimately serve no purpose other than restricting a great deal of activity and forcing me to subsist on macaroni and cheese? Utilizing Thorstein Veblen's *Theory of the Leisure Class*, I will address this question in two parts: 1) Why is conspicuous and wasteful consumption on the part of women encouraged; and specifically, why do I buy at Victoria's Secret when I could get comparable items at discount outlets such as TJ Maxx; and 2) why restrictive lingerie reaffirms traditional gender roles in our society.

Veblen details women's role in the concept of conspicuous consumption as that of a trophy, or ornament, for a man's household; "she is petted, and is permitted, or even required, to consume largely and conspicuously—vicariously for her husband or other natural guardian. She is exempted, or debarred, from vulgarly useful employment—in order to perform leisure vicariously for the good repute of her natural (pecuniary) guardian" (p. 232). In other words, women function mainly to uphold the position of men in society; their consumption and leisure reflect the ability of their spouses to provide for the household. Even today, when women do engage in work outside the home and contribute handsomely to the household income, their consumption patterns can be seen as evidence of how well her husband is doing. This is due in part to the fact that women earn far less than men in comparable work situations, and males in a two-income family generally provide the greater amount of money. If women do not work, their leisure is veritable proof that their husbands are successful (i.e. demonstrate the "prowess" of old).

The Baby Boomers of today are such good examples of conspicuous consumption, it's laughable (of course, I'm referring to the "Yuppies," but I hate that term and prefer not to use it). They are the new "leisure class," and the standards of living that they set are emulated throughout society. Even though it would appear that the "Y-word" heyday is over, it is safe to assume that consumption patterns that American society has become accustomed to will persist; "It frequently happens that an element of the standard of living which set out with being primarily wasteful, ends with becoming, in the apprehension of the consumer, a necessity of life; and it may in this way become as indispensable as any other item of the consumer's habitual expenditure" (p. 79). As society goes, so go I; and my conspicuously wasteful habit of purchasing lingerie will doubtlessly continue for years.

Why, then, do I not scale down my purchases and, for instance, buy imitation silks or functionally appropriate pieces at a discount store? Veblen answers, "The superior gratification derived from the use and contemplation of costly and supposedly beautiful products, is commonly, in great measure a gratification of our sense of costliness masquerading under the name of beauty" (p. 95). It almost seems facile—of course expensive equals beautiful! Polyester went the way of the 70s for the most part, to reappear today as very pricey "rayon" garments. If anyone had told me years ago that I'd pay just as much for synthetics as for silks, I would not have believed them. As it happens, rayon is expensive, therefore acceptable (and in my closet). More to the point, I buy lingerie at Victoria's Secret because it seems, somehow, better. I live on macaroni and cheese because of it, but Veblen tells me that "people will undergo a very considerable degree of privation in the comforts or the necessities of life in order to appear well dressed" (p. 119).

This brings me to my second main point, which centers around how lingerie, which is not visible to the world at large, fits into the concept of conspicuous consumption; and further, why wearing lingerie that is beautiful but horribly uncomfortable reaffirms traditional gender roles.

It is an indisputable assertion that women today are a work force of their own. They are engaged in every aspect of labor, from blue collar to the boardroom. Even so, women are required to go inflexibly from the boardroom to the bedroom, and it is there that a lot of equality is lost. It remains in some people's heads that somehow women aren't "supposed" to work, as they were required not to in Veblen's leisure class. Popular advertisements for Maidenform lingerie tout "The Hidden Side of the Girl in the Gray Flannel Suit," which is offensive for many reasons, not the least of which is the use of the term *girl*. What ads like this infer is that even though a woman might be out in the working world, wearing sexless suits and exhibiting traditionally masculine traits, underneath she is still a frivolous plaything. Lingerie can be included in the category of various "mutilations" which Veblen calls "items of pecuniary and cultural beauty which we have come to do duty as elements of the ideal of womanliness" (p. 108).

It is when a woman returns home from work and takes on her second job of creating a sanctuary for her mate that she can create the illusion of "a relation of economic dependence; a relation which in the last analysis must, in economic theory, reduce itself to a relation of servitude" (p. 127). The ideal of femininity and "womanliness" is tied up intrinsically with her ability to be a soft, incapable trophy for her master. A quick look at any magazine geared toward male fantasies will show that images of helplessness (bondage?) abound, and the current popularity of such items as merry widow and camisettes reinforce this ideal. Without going into details, both of the aforementioned garments are very expensive, uncomfortable, and restrictive pieces of lingerie that are reminiscent of the corset. Suffice it to say that they both are formed with metal, and I own some.

The fact that hundreds of women today wear corsetlike garments does not in itself make them totally incapable of productive labor (semi-incapable, but not totally), rather it serves to reinforce the private illusion that the man is, indeed, the worker and the provider. The whole world doesn't have to see evidence of her infirmities, as that certainly goes against current societal norms, but at home (where a "man's home is his castle") "the womanliness of women's apparel resolves itself, in point of substantial fact, into the more effective hindrance to useful exertion offered by the garments peculiar to women" (p. 121). The more tangible evidence shown of a woman's femininity (as traditionally defined), the more reassured a man is that he is, above all, definitively masculine. The consumption of expensive and restrictive lingerie conforms to "the general rule . . . that women should consume only for the benefit of their masters" (p. 63). The fact that I do it is, in my mind, comparable to others forms of deviant and destructive behavior, but we'll keep it our little secret. My friends in Women's Studies would surely string me up by my heels, but as I look at it, admitting there's a problem is the first step to recovery.

Sarajane's essay is rich in its coherent understanding of not only her own behavior, but that of many women in her culture. Like Bender, Sarajane needed to study the object she was drawn to in order to understand what the object was steering her toward. Once she understood the effect, she could choose to limit its impact.

CONCLUSION

An overarching need in the use of images for insight is the development of one's capability to use art rather than to criticize it. Sarajane did not critique Veblen, she used his theories; Bender did not admire Amish quilts, she applied their lessons to her daily life. The same holds true for the use of writing or language for insight. We need to use what seems useless: Art and images do not appear practical, and, yet, both Bender and Sarajane used them to come to insight. The inversion of what is useful and useless are best expressed in the words of playwright Eugene Ionesco as quoted by Merton in his essay "Rain and the Rhinoceros" in Merton's (1964) most creative book *Raids on the Unspeakable*:

> The universal and modern man is the man in a rush (i.e. a rhinoceros), a man who has no time, who is a prisoner of necessity, who cannot understand that a thing might perhaps be without usefulness; nor does he understand that, at bottom, it is the useful that may be a useless and back-breaking burden. If one does not understand the usefulness of the useless and the uselessness of the useful, one cannot understand art. And a country where art is not understood is a country of slaves and robots. . . ." (*Notes et Contre Notes*, p. 129). Rhinoceritis, he adds, is the sickness that lies in wait "for those who *have lost the sense and the taste for solitude.*" (p. 21)

In the college classroom, the "usefulness" of first-year composition and the emphasis in arts classes on "critiques" should, in Ionesco's terms, be seen as in part a refusal to participate in the reflection that meaningful scholarship and composing require. Instead, the solitude (and it is possible, claimed Miles, to have a collective solitude in the contemplation of an image) required to stir wonderings, to allow the intuition to lead, and to rest in contemplation of an image must be given space in college classrooms. Until such room is given—in assignments and in writing—Ernest Boyer's dream of synthesis and integration in higher education will never come about.

Educational researchers who share Boyer's concern note the thicket that educators are in as a whole: Standardized assessments drive attention away from reflection, while the way the scores are interpreted ignores the person of both the student and the teacher (Moss, 1994). This book—in its attempts to enlarge the understanding of insight and to provide two measurement instruments for insight in writing—is a beginning, a way to focus attention on the experience of insight that requires inquiry, reflection, and attention to complexity with the full human person.

Educators call for the development of thinking through collaborative inquiry to meet the needs of our changing global economy. And the advances made by those who are willing to attempt insight are evident in the collaborative efforts of business and industry. Kazuma Tateisi, who founded Omron Sun House, outside Kyoto, Japan, is one such person (Goleman, Kaufman, & Ray, 1992). By integrating systems theory from engineering with the needs of the severely handicapped, he adapted machines in his very successful high-tech company to the physical capabilities of each worker, thereby enabling each one to offer what they can to society. Whole assembly lines reach down to workers' wheelchairs, and the machines correspond to the efforts of each individual. It is Tateisi's innovative thinking that fostered interdependence, in enabling each person to contribute to the whole.

To focus on insight in writing in the college classroom—through attention to and reflection on ideas or images—is to transform the seemingly useless into the useful and to work in a meaningful way with the art that resides in our minds and issues forth from our hands. Although insight remains a mystery in its origins, its process of coming into being, and its appearances, it holds a fundamental place in college education. The search for it alone indicates a willingness to admit complexity, which is essential for any good scholarship.

Paradox is a staple of the spiritual world, as it is a staple of insight. It asks students to hold simultaneously an active concern for dissonance with a reflective poise and a whole-personed response. Out of such interplay and paradox insights come. In a culture such as ours, in which facts, activity, and testing prevent such paradox, they also prevent insight. The spiritual malaise of higher education, so well described by Belenky et al. (1986), Bellah et al. (1991), Fox (1988), and Smith (1990), can only be remedied by the paradoxes that foster insight because within insight is the unification and harmony of the human person that can blossom in direction, responsibility, and peace.

References

Asher, J.W. (1976). *Educational research and evaluation methods.* Boston: Little Brown.

Baltazar, E.R. (1966). *Teilhard and the supernatural.* Baltimore, MD: Helicon.

Bandura, A. (1965, April). *Psychotherapy conceptualized as a social-learning process.* Paper presented at the Kentucky Centennial Symposium on Psychotherapy, University of Kentucky, Lexington.

Batson, C., Ventis, D., & Ventis, W.L. (1982). *The religious experience.* New York: Oxford University Press.

Baum, G. (1973). Foreword. In A.M. Greeley (Ed.), *New agenda* (pp. 25-29). Garden City, NY: Paulist Press.

Beck, A.T., Rush, A.J., Shaw, B.F., & Emery, G. (1979). *Cognitive therapy of depression.* New York: Guilford Press.

Belenky, M.F., Clinchy, B.M., Goldberger, N.R., & Tarule, J.M. (1986). *Women's ways of knowing.* New York: Basic Books.

Bellah, R.N., Madsen, R., Sullivan, W.M., Swidler, A., & Tipton, S.M. (1985). *Habits of the heart: Individualism and commitment in American life.* New York: Harper & Row.

Bellah, R.N., Madsen, R., Sullivan, W.M., Swidler, A., & Tipton, S.M. (1991). *The good society.* New York: Alfred A. Knopf.

Bender, S. (1989). *Plain and simple.* San Francisco: HarperSanFrancisco.

Berlin, J.A. (1984). *Writing instruction in nineteenth-century colleges.* Carbondale, IL: Southern Illinois University Press.

Berlin, J.A. (1990). Writing instruction in school and college English, 1890-1985. In J.J. Murphy (Ed.), *A short history of writing instruction* (pp. 183-220). Davis, CA: Hermagoras Press.

Berthoff, A. (1981). *The making of meaning: Metaphors, models, and maxims for writing teachers.* Montclair, NJ: Boyton/ Cook.

Blum, H. (1979). The curative and creative aspects of insight. *Journal of the American Psychoanalytic Association, 27* (Suppl. 41-69).

Boyer, E.L. (1987). *College: The undergraduate experience in America.* New York: Harper & Row.

Brady, J. (1967). Psychotherapy, learning theory, and insight. *Archives of General Psychiatry, 16,* 304-311.

Braio, F. P. (1988). *Lonergan's retrieval of the notion of human being.* Lanham, MD: University Press of America.

Bruner, J. (1963). *On knowing.* Cambridge, MA: Belknap Press.

Bultmann, R. (1961). *Kerygma and myth.* New York: Harper & Row.

Cronbach, L.J. (1988). Five perspectives on the validity argument. In R. Wainer & H.I. Braun (Eds.), *Test validity* (pp. 3-17). Hillsdale, NJ: Lawrence Erlbaum Associates.

Daly, J., & Miller., M. (1975). Identifying students who are anxious about writing and the empirical development of an instrument to measure writing apprehension. *Research in the Teaching of English, 9,* 242-249.

D'Angelo, F.J. (1975). *A conceptual theory of rhetoric.* Englewood Cliffs, NJ: Winthrop.

De Bono, E. (1970). *Lateral thinking: Creativity step by step.* New York: Harper Colophon.

De Bono, E. (1992). *Serious creativity.* New York: HarperBusiness.

de Man, P. (1983). *Blindness and insight* (2nd ed). Minneapolis: University of Minnesota Press.

Diederich, P. (1974). *Measuring growth in English.* Urbana, IL: National Council of Teachers of English.

Dulles, A. (1985). Model five: Revelation as new awareness. In *Models of revelation* (pp. 98-114). New York: Doubleday.

Elbow, P. (1973). *Writing without teachers.* New York: Oxford University Press.

Elbow, P. (1981). *Writing with power.* New York: Oxford University Press.

Elbow, P. (1986). *Embracing contraries.* New York: Oxford University Press.

Elliott, R. (1983). Fitting process research to the practicing psychotherapist. *Psychotherapy: Theory, Research, and Practice, 20*, 47-55.

Elliott, R. (1985). Helpful and nonhelpful events in brief counseling interviews: An empirical taxonomy. *Journal of Counseling Psychology, 32*, 307-322.

Elliott, R., James, E., Reimschuessel, C., Cislo, D, & Sack, N. (1985). Significant events and the analysis of immediate therapeutic impacts. *Psychotherapy, 22*, 620-630.

Elliott, R., Reimschuessel, C., Sack, N., Cislo, D., & James, E. (1984). *Therapeutic impacts content analysis system: Rating manual.* Unpublished manuscript, Department of Psychology, University of Toledo.

Emig, J. (1977). Writing as a mode of learning. *College Composition and Communication, 28*, 122-128.

Erikson, E. (1964). *Insight and responsibility.* New York: Norton.

Fawcett, T. (1971). *The symbolic language of religion.* Minneapolis, MN: Augsburg.

Fenishel, O. (1945). *The psychoanalytic theory of neurosis.* New York: Norton.

Festinger, L. (1957). *A theory of cognitive dissonance.* Stanford, CA: Stanford University Press.

Finley, J. (1978). *Merton's palace of nowhere.* Notre Dame, IN: Ave Maria Press.

Flower, L., & Hayes, J.R. (1980). The cognition of discovery: Defining a rhetorical problem. *College Composition and Communication, 31*, 21-32.

Flower, L., & Hayes, J. R. (1981). A cognitive process theory of writing. *College Composition and Communication, 32*, 365-387.

Fontinell, E. (1970). *Toward a reconstruction of religion.* Garden City, NY: Doubleday.

Fox, M. (1988). *The coming of the cosmic Christ.* New York: Harper & Row.

Freire, P. (1982). *Pedagogy of the oppressed.* New York: Continuum.

Gates, R. (1989). Applying Michael Greenspan's concept of insight to composition theory. *Journal of Advanced Compositioon, 9*, 59-68.

Gates, R. (1993). Creativity and insight: Toward a poetics of composition. In A.R. Gere (Ed.), *Into the field: Sites of composition studies* (pp. 147-158). New York: Modern Language

Association.

Geisinger, K.F. (1992). The metamorphosis of test validation. *Educational Psychologist, 27*, 197-222.

Gerzon, M. (1982). *A choice of heroes*. Boston: Houghton Mifflin.

Glass, G. (1986). Testing old, testing new: Schoolboy psychology and the allocation of intellectual resources. In B.S. Plake & J.C. Witt (Eds.), *The future of testing* (pp. 9-27). Hillsdale, NJ: Lawrence Erlbaum Associates.

Goleman, D., Kaufman, P., & Ray, M. (1992). *The creative spirit*. New York: Dutton.

Gould, S.J. (1981). *The mismeasure of man*. New York: Norton.

Guilford, J.P. (1967). Creativity: Yesterday, today, and tomorrow. *Journal of Creative Behavior, 1*, 3-8.

Hillman, J. & Ventura, M. (1992). *We've had a hundred years of psychotherapy—and the world's getting worse*. New York: HarperCollins.

Hillocks, G. (1984). What works in teaching composition: A meta-analysis of experimental treatment studies. *American Journal of Education, 93*, 133-170.

James, W. (1929). *The varieties of religious experience*. New York: Modern Library (Original work published 1902).

Johnson, D.L. (1979). *Creativity checklist*. Chicago, IL: Stoeling.

Kagan, N. (1975). *Interpersonal process recall: A method of influencing human interaction*. (Available from N. Kagan, 434 Erickson Hall, College of Education, Michigan State University, East Lansing, MI, 48824.)

Kerlinger, F.N. (1986). *Foundations of behavioral research* (3rd ed.). New York: Holt, Rinehart, & Winston.

Klein, M., Mathieu, P.L., Gendlin, E.T., & Kiesler, D.J. (1969). *The experiencing scale: A research and training manual* (Vol. 1). Madison, WI: Wisconsin Psychiatric Institute.

Koestler, A. (1949). *Insight and outlook*. New York: Macmillan.

Kroll, B. (1980). Developmental perspectives and the teaching of composition. *College English, 41*, 741-752.

Labov, W., & Fanshel, D. (1977). *Therapeutic discourse: Psychotherapy as conversation*. New York: Academic Press.

Langer, J.A., & Applebee, A.N. (1987). *How writing shapes thinking*. Urbana, IL: National Council of Teachers of English.

Lauer, J.M. (1967). *Invention in contemporary rhetoric: Heuristic procedures*. Unpublished doctoral dissertation, University of Michigan, East Lansing.

Lauer, J.M. (1982). Writing as inquiry: Some questions for teachers. *College Composition and Communication, 33*, 89-93.

Lauer, J.M., Montague, G., Emig, J., & Lunsford, A. (1991). *Four worlds of writing* (3rd ed.). New York: HarperCollins.

London, P. (1964). *The modes and morals of psychotherapy.* New York: Holt, Rinehart, & Winston.

Lonergan, B. (1978). *Insight: A study in human understanding.* New York: Philosophical Library. (Original work published in 1957.)

Lunsford, A. (1979). Cognitive development and the basic writer. *College English, 41,* 38-46.

Lunsford, A. (1980). The content of basic writers' essays. *College Composition and Communication, 31,* 278-290.

Macrorie, K. (1968). To be read. *English Journal, 57,* 686-692.

Mahrer, A.R. (1985). *Psychotherapeutic change: An alternative approach to meaning and measurement.* New York: Norton.

Mathieu-Coughlan, P., & Klein, M. (1984). Experiential psychotherapy: Key events in client-therapist interaction. In L.N. Rice & L.S. Greenberg (Eds.), *Patterns of change* (pp. 213-248). New York: Guilford.

McFague, S. (1987). *Models of God.* Philadelphia: Fortress Press.

Meichenbaum, D. (1977). *Cognitive behavior modification.* New York: Plenum.

Mendel, W.M. (1975). Interpretation and working through. *American Journal of Psychotherapy, 29,* 409-414.

Merton, T. (1953). *The sign of Jonas.* San Diego: Harvest/Harcourt Brace Jovanovich.

Merton, T. (1955). *No man is an island.* San Diego: Harvest/Harcourt Brace Jovanovich.

Merton, T. (1964). *Raids on the unspeakable.* New York: New Directions.

Merton, T. (1973). Final integration. In T. Merton (Ed.), *Contemplation in a world of action* (pp. 172-179). New York: Image.

Messick, S. (1988). The once and future issues of validity: Assessing meaning and consequences of measurement. In R. Wainer & H.I. Braun (Eds.), *Test validity* (pp. 33-45). Hillsdale, NJ: Lawrence Erlbaun Associates.

Messick, S. (1989). Meaning and values in test validation: The science and ethics of assessment. *Educational Researcher, 18,* 5-11.

Miles, M. (1985). *Image as insight.* Boston: Beacon.

Miller, A. (1981). *The drama of the gifted child.* (R. Ward, Trans.). New York: Basic.

Moss, P.A. (1994). Can there be validity without reliability? *Educational Researcher, 23*, 5-12.

Murray, D.M. (1985). *A writer teaches writing* (2nd ed.). Boston: Houghton Mifflin.

Murray, M.M. (1987). *Measuring insight in student writing.* Unpublished doctoral dissertation, Purdue University, West Lafayette, IN.

Neubauer, P. (1979). The role of insight in psychoanalysis. *Journal of the American Psychoanalytic Association, 27* (Suppl. 29-40).

Noy, P. (1978). Insight and creativity. *Journal of the American Psychoanalytic Association, 26,* 717-748.

Nunnally, J. (1978). *Psychometric theory* (2nd ed.). New York: McGraw-Hill.

Odell, L. (1981). Defining and assessing competence in writing. In C. Cooper (Ed.), *The nature and measurement of competency in English* (pp. 95-138). Urbana, IL: National Council of Teachers of English.

Ohlsson, S. (1984). Restructuring revisited: An information processing theory of restructuring and insight. *Scandinavian Journal of Psychology, 25*, 117-129.

O'Meara, T.F. (1975). Toward a subjective theology of revelation. *Theological Studies, 26*, 401-427.

O'Meara, T.F. (1990). *Fundamentalism: A Catholic perspective.* New York: Paulist Press.

Perkins, D.N. (1981). *The mind's best work.* Cambridge, MA: Harvard University Press.

Perl, S. (1978). *Five writers writing: Case studies of the composing processes of unskilled college writers.* Unpublished doctoral dissertation, New York University, New York.

Piaget, J. (1968). *Six psychological studies.* New York: Vintage Press.

Quellmalz, E.S. (1981, August). *Issues in designing instructional research: Examples from research on writing competence.* Paper presented at the annual meeting of the American Psychological Association, Los Angeles.

Rahner, K. (1966). Observations on the concept of revelation. In K. Rahner & J. Ratzinger (Eds.), *Revelation and tradition* (pp. 9-25). New York: Herder & Herder.

Reich, R. (1992). *The work of nations: Preparing ourselves for twenty-first century capitalism.* New York: Vintage Press.

Roback, H.B. (1974). Insight: A bridging of the theoretical and research literature. *The Canadian Psychologist, 15*, 61-89.

Rokeach, M. (1979). Value education in educational settings. In M. Rokeach (Ed.), *Understanding human values: Individual and societal* (pp. 259-269). New York: The Free Press.

Rothenberg, A. (1979, June). Creative contradictions. *Psychology Today,* pp. 55-62.

Schaef, A. W. (1992). *Beyond therapy, beyond science: A new model for healing the whole person.* San Francisco: HarperSanFrancisco.

Schafer, R. (1978). *Language and insight.* New Haven, CT: Yale University Press.

Schonbar, R. (1965). Interpretation and insight in psychotherapy. *Psychotherapy: Theory, Research, and Practice, 2,* 78-84.

Searle, J. R. (1969). *Speech acts: An essay in the philosophy of language.* London: Cambridge University Press.

Segal, H. (1962). The curative factors in psychoanalysis. *International Journal of Psychoanalysis, 43,* 212-217.

Shea, J. (1980). *Stories of faith.* Chicago: Thomas More Press.

Shengold, L. (1981). Insight as metaphor. *Psychoanalytic Study of the Child, 36,* 289-306.

Sloan, D. (1983). *Insight-imagination.* Westport, CT: Greenwood Press.

Smith, P. (1990). *Killing the spirit.* New York: Penguin.

Snyder, W. U. (1945). An investigation of the nature of non-directive psychotherapy. *Journal of General Psychology, 33,* 193-223.

Strupp, H. H., & Binder, J. C. (1984). *Psychotherapy in a new key.* New York: Basic Books.

Tavris, C. (1992). *The mismeasure of woman.* New York: Simon & Schuster.

Thurston, L. L. (1959). *The measurement of values.* Chicago: University of Chicago Press.

Tillich, P. (1951). *Systematic theology* (Vol. 1). Chicago: University of Chicago Press.

Torrance, E. P. (1970). *Encouraging creativity in the classroom.* Dubuque, IA: William C. Brown.

Wallas, G. (1926). *The art of thought.* New York: Random House.

Wallerstein, R. (1983). Some thoughts about insight and psychoanalysis. *Israel Journal of Psychiatry and Related Sciences, 20,* 33-43.

Waskow, I. E., & Parloff, M. B. (1975). *Psychotherapy change measures.* Rockville, MD: National Institute of Mental Health.

Weiner, I. B. (1975). *Principles of psychotherapy.* New York:

Wiley.

Westerman, M. A. (1989). A naturalized view of the role played by insight. *Journal of Integrative & Eclectic Psychotherapy, 8,* 197-221.

White, E.M. (1985). *Teaching and assessing writing.* San Francisco: Jossey-Bass.

Young, R. (1978). Paradigms and problems: Needed research in rhetorical invention. In C. Cooper & L. Odell (Eds.), *Points of departure* (pp. 29-47). Urbana, IL: National Council of Teachers of English.

Young, R. (1980). Arts, crafts, gifts, and knacks: Some disharmonies in the new rhetoric. *Visible Language, 14,* 341-350.

Young, R., Becker, A., & Pike, K. (1970). *Rhetoric: Discovery and change.* New York: Harcourt Brace Jovanovich.

Author Index

Subject Index